WHEN THEY
COME BACK MISSING

When They Come Back Missing

Wanda Hawblitzel

Copyright © 2015 by Wanda Hawblitzel.

Library of Congress Control Number:		2015914961
ISBN:	Hardcover	978-1-5144-0683-0
	Softcover	978-1-5144-0682-3
	eBook	978-1-5144-0681-6

All rights reserved. No part of this book may be reproduced or transmitted in any form or by any means, electronic or mechanical, including photocopying, recording, or by any information storage and retrieval system, without permission in writing from the copyright owner.

Any people depicted in stock imagery provided by Thinkstock are models, and such images are being used for illustrative purposes only. Certain stock imagery © Thinkstock.

Print information available on the last page.

Rev. date: 10/09/2015

To order additional copies of this book, contact:
Xlibris
1-888-795-4274
www.Xlibris.com
Orders@Xlibris.com
720904

Contents

Acknowledgment vii

Faithful but Not Spared 1
The Price of Silence 21
In an Instant . . . He Was Gone 56
Entitled 69
Closing 80

Acknowledgment

I would like to thank a few people for their encouragement and support throughout the process of writing this book. . There were many times when I wanted to quit and walk away. Their encouraging words often reminded me of why I started this project and pushed me to finish something that was so very close to my heart.

First I would like to thank my children for their never-ending love and support. They mean the world to me and I am very proud of the type of adults they have become.

The words "Thank you" does not seem to be enough for my friend Joe Sullivan. He was a huge support to me personally and also during the book writing process. He, an extremely talented individual, shared his talent with me by providing the image for my book cover. Thank you for your friendship.

Thank you so much to Kelly Morrison for her time reading and rereading. Your guidance and suggestions as to direction with the book was deeply appreciated.

Finally I would like to thank the wives that shared their stories with me so that I could share mine. Your contribution enabled me to tell others of an emotional unexplainable loss that not only affected me but others.

There is a rising epidemic in our nation, one that tears families apart and destroys the mental well-being of honorable and noble soldiers. Soldiers that return home and are slowly dismantling, mentally, with every deployment they complete. The inability to cope with day-to-day life and becoming emotionally disconnected are now challenges some of them face. Unprepared families suffer in a struggle to understand and cope with the postwar soldier. A completed deployment and a successful mission are sadly now at the sacrifice of the family.

These families stand by and watch as their soldier trains for a mission in great strength and detail. This is a mission that we, the family, become attached to and pray for nothing but its success. For when we have a successful mission completed, we in return get our soldier back. That is the main hope and goal that soldiers and their families focus on. A hope of their return home and mistakenly, we have expected their full return.

As a military family living in a time of unending war, life is fast-paced in an undated wait for the return home of our soldiers fighting this war. We are the wives, husbands, children, mothers, and fathers to a new version of an American hero. We are just as strong as we are weak. Tears that get suppressed in order to complete another day closer to their return are a common practice for us. Days consist of counting down to a date, that is not even definite, living on hope and being a main support for a soldier that needs you during this time. We are mothers now fathers and fathers now being mothers. We suffer inside and physically ache not only from separation but fear of the unknown and its ability to become part of your being. It is a fear that does not leave us until they return home. We are a care package from home, a video chat at night, informative e-mail and long awaited phone call. We are main supports for them, and the thought of us is what keeps them going in this time of war. The return home is now their goal, and we are here waiting.

Faithful but Not Spared

Divorce itself is a traumatic event in one's life. It can change the way you think, your tolerance levels, and make you more aware emotionally. If you add the responsibility of two children and knowing you are now a single parent, you can imagine what one's expectations must have been for a new relationship, yet alone a second marriage.

My first marriage blessed me with two wonderful children. It was just the three of us and I was not interested in dating unless I felt like someone could step in and possibly be the right man for not only me but also for my children. I was not going to jump into anything. I wanted to take it slow and make sure with God and prayer, the right man would be presented to me and I would just know that he was the one.

I, a woman deeply devoted to my faith, made it a priority in my life and God always came first. I knew that the day I did meet someone special, it was going to have God's hand in it from the beginning. I had been introduced to a man through mutual friends at our church. We spoke often and this led to the approach of a first date. Prior to our first date, I found myself on my knees asking God for guidance, fasting, and consulting my pastor. I needed to do this before making the decision to go out with him. All of this was part of my faith and helping me choose a man not only for me, but one that would be there for my children. On our very first date, we made a huge connection. We actually ended our date by praying together. It was so important that he had taken my hand and prayed with me that evening. I really felt this could be the man God wanted for my family. He in turn, felt the same way about me.

He was not stationed here at the time and had been deployed three times even before I met him. He had not been in the service too long and had been in a heavy rotation between stateside assignments and three war zones. One of these war zones was Afghanistan and the other two were to Iraq. He had basically spent more time overseas than he did here in the United States.

Before his last deployment he had grown closer to the Lord and became saved through our church. He was a man of strong faith now and I was very attracted to him. When he returned from that deployment, he did not return here but was sent to a course that he needed to complete. We continued to date long distance talking on the phone and every night we would pray together before we went to bed. Again, we connected spiritually and this was very important to me when looking for a man to spend the rest of my life with. I felt just as strong that he wanted the same in a woman that he would one day marry.

We started dating in November and married in March. Yes, it all happened very quickly. Did I mention I was not going to jump into anything and wanted to take things slow? That right there should tell you I was surely positive about this man, his faith, and his love for me. I was at ease with this decision to marry because God was still the center of our home. God was the rock on which we were building our marriage and felt our union was good. Do not get me wrong; there were a few things we were trying to work out. He was an opinionated self-confident man and I knew that was exactly what the military looked for, arrogant self-confident men that were not afraid. A lot of women are attracted to that also and I guess I was one of them. He had no children so my children were an issue. The father of my children was not nice or easy to work with. This created problems but we were working on them. We would talk about the issues. We would share our feelings and thoughts about the matter, and all of our discussions, always ended with prayer. We had come from very different backgrounds. Economically and traditionally, our lives were completely different. Combining our lives, realizing the expectations each of us had for the marriage and family . . . these were things I knew we still needed to work through. We were communicating well and did what married couples do to resolve issues.

He had taken command as a captain the same month we were married. I took over the FRG (Family Readiness Group) while working full-time and raising two kids. The FRG was in total disarray and the men were gearing up to deploy in October. Those next six months were hectic. It was emotionally draining on me to help prepare these women for the deployment of their husbands. I was to lead them and help guide them through this process, all the while preparing my family for the deployment of my own husband. He himself was preparing the soldiers for deployment and training was nonstop. This was a struggle as a newly married couple and there were disagreements but he had always been there to talk me through them. He would ask if we could just sit down and talk it out, telling me that communication is the number one thing in a marriage and that we can pray through this. He was very sensitive to what I needed in a husband and made it a point to be that man for me. He wanted to do this for me and I loved that about him.

Throughout our short courtship and marriage, he was very romantic with me. I recall him saying things to me that would turn my emotions and feelings into a whirlpool of a schoolgirl smitten and an adult woman in love. He had handwritten notes telling me of how blessed he was and how much he loved me. I would receive e-mails from him at random, referencing his love for not only me but for my children. He did all those things you look for in a man and gave me special moments that made me realize he loved me. I knew we had difficulties, but God was still the center of our lives and I knew we could work through them. I had no doubts. I was positive about our marriage and our love for each other and knew we would make it as a couple.

He left again at the end of September (beginning of October) to start his fourth deployment. By November, he had already lost one soldier to an IED. It exploded during his convoy. He had made a decision on which way to go and that route resulted in the loss of his strongest lieutenant, his "right-hand man." Another soldier was burned over 80 percent of his body and another sustained severe injuries. He had to physically carry one of his soldiers to the helicopter in order for them to receive medical attention and be evacuated. He saw all of it happen up close and very personal. As the commander, he dealt with the fallout from this incident and I dealt with the FRG part of it back home. Yet through this and the deployment it seemed like our communication was still very strong. He was not praying with me, but I was on my knees daily praying him through that deployment. You see, he had stopped praying with me when he deployed. His excuse was that others might see or hear him. He was the captain. He could not have that. He was dealing with some ongoing issues with soldiers at the time and it was a hard command so, I did not push it. He would call almost every day to talk to me, check on the kids and make sure we were doing well. I fully intended to fall back into the routine of praying with him again, upon his return home, and was certain he wanted the same.

Life back home did not stop although at times it felt that way. We had started the process of building a house. When I say house, I mean our dream home. I noticed when we spoke at times, he would get a little angry and be unreasonable about certain things pertaining to the new house. I just chalked it up to him not being here and not being able to see what the process was first hand, more or less just frustration about making decisions from so far away.

We were very excited about his return home for midtour and everything was great in that two-week process of R&R (R&R, Rest and Relaxation, Midtour). During his time home, he was determined to pay a visit to his soldier that had been burned in that convoy explosion. He was insisting on presenting him personally with a military certificate. He was adamant about doing this and wanted me to go with him. The whole trip we planned was focused on visiting this soldier. He was determined to get to this soldier and present him with this certificate, yet my husband left the certificate at home. I did not quite understand what he was thinking at the time and it was confusing. I can only guess that it was not really about the certificate at all. I think that he felt the need to physically see this soldier again, to be able to touch him and know that he was going to recover. My parents had it overnighted to us and he was able to fulfill a personal mission that he felt he needed to do so badly.

He was only home two weeks. It was easy to get along for two weeks. My children were not there at the time and R&R went well. I did notice he was not interested in knowing what we had been doing or the progress that had been made on the house. We did pick out some things together for the house but not much discussion went on about the process. My children joined us toward the end of his R&R and the time spent was taken as a gift. We were blessed to have these moments with him at home during a year of such uncertainty.

His deployment was supposed to be a fifteen-month tour but it ended at thirteen months. We were excited about his early return. That does not happen often and we were blessed. My husband was coming home and we were thrilled. He returned in October and instantly, I knew he had been returned to us as a shell of his former self. It was not a slow "here and there notes of difference," it was instant. The night he returned, we did the reunion and welcome-home ceremony on base and went home to our new house. He just walked in and went to a different room in what I can only describe as a mental disconnect. It was like he did not even want to be with us. He just wanted to be on the couch watching TV, alone. There was no communication, just silence.

Within the next few weeks his behavior was unable to be comprehended. He would sleep a lot. He ate peanut butter and jelly sandwiches every day for two months. He would not sit down to a meal, just peanut butter and jelly sandwiches. He could not sit still. He would go from the computer to the kitchen to the TV, repeatedly. He refused to pray with me. When I asked, something that was once so important to the both of us, he refused. When he returned home, I wanted to fall back into that routine with him and he was not willing.

I loved church, my pastor, and Sunday service. He did too, after all that is where we had met. Getting him to attend became a struggle. If we did attend he was constantly asking me, during service, what time it was, where was my watch, where was my phone? He would continuously check the time. As I sat there listening to the sermon he would lean over and ask me if I wanted coffee. He would offer repeatedly to go get it for me. I felt as though I was trying to keep a child pacified during church. He clearly did not want to be there and sitting amongst that amount of people for an hour was too much for him.

He was unable to stay in one place for very long. He was extremely agitated and traveling from one thing to the next; fifteen minutes on the computer, twenty minutes in front of the TV, bouncing from one task to another never calming down. He went from sleeping a lot to not much at all. With the exception of that first two weeks home, he did not sleep unless he was completely exhausted. This behavior became his demeanor and his way of life.

I tried my best to reconnect with him and reach out. Unaware of what he was dealing with, I could only offer being a wife to him and my love. I soon learned that would not be enough. One incident I recall vividly, my husband was sitting at the computer and I came up behind him. I was not being secretive or quiet I just walked up behind him. He did not hear me. I touched him slowly as to run my fingers over his head. He reacted quickly and combatively by throwing himself instantly at me and nearly knocking me out. His eyes were full of fear yet determination, as though he were ready to battle. It was me though, his wife, could he not see that? I was standing there confused and shocked at his reaction but realizing I myself was in a battle. I wanted my husband back and I was going to fight for him. At that moment, I tried to push him to talk to me. I kept asking him "Why won't you talk to me?" It just angered him that much more. Shortly after this incident, I had pushed him verbally to open up to me. I kept asking him to communicate with me, to express to me what he was feeling and why he felt the need to push me away. He became so angry with me, that he said "Why don't you just leave me the fuck alone? Just one fucking minute alone?" This was from a man who did not use that word yet, used it every day upon his return.

I, the woman he loved so much, was bearing the brunt of his anger. While he was deployed, I begged God for his safe return and to keep and protect him. He came back with an obvious mental struggle that I did not understand. I did not know how to help him so again, I did the one thing I knew how to do and I prayed for his safe return.

Our relationship became contemptuous and explosive. There were many more arguments. Our disagreements were mostly about the children, my ex-husband, and finances. If I bought a book, he would ask why. He would state that we needed that extra money for more important needs. The confrontation then would turn, always, to the less fortunate in Iraq. He would ask if I realized that there were people in Iraq that had nothing yet I went and bought this book, CD, or whatever he was arguing at that moment. He would demean me for buying what he considered a luxury. Of course I would remind him that I worked and that if I wanted to purchase a book, then I would . . . and from there we would end up in full-blown arguments, arguments that did not need to be argued. He could not appreciate the way we lived. He stated often, "I saw people who have nothing yet you live in this great splendor." Life for me became, tip toeing around letting things go and not arguing things I might have disputed before. I was at the point that if I went to buy a book, I would think about it first and consider if it was really worth the argument I knew would result from its purchase. I would second-guess my everyday normal. I was living like this, because I had no idea how he would react or how my actions might set him off.

His statements, reactions, and logic became so extreme. He said things like "The kids didn't need Christmas gifts." His thinking was if they did not need them, why should we buy them. We should only be buying things they needed not items they wanted. It did not matter that this would make them happy on Christmas day. In his mind, they did not need it, so therefore we should not buy them anything. His logic and views were the same for their birthdays too. Nothing he said made sense to me anymore and when he spoke I often wondered who was speaking to me. I tried to process what was happening but confusion was in control of me and my life with him was a daily change.

My children watched the change in him take over our lives. His daily battles affected them and the relationship they had developed with him as their stepfather. My daughter interacted with him well. Prior to deployment, he did things with her, laughed and played. They had their own code and words for things. They enjoyed each other and he was good to her. Their closeness faded upon his return. It was not the same and she knew he was not the same. She escaped the brunt of his anger and it was never aimed at her. When it came to my son though, he would say, "He needs to be a man, grow up, have more responsibility and do things a man would do. He needs to stop crying and take responsibility." With my daughter it was "I love you"; with my son it was "He doesn't need to hear it from me." Part of that I think, was how he was raised but it became more intense with his return from deployment. I know his job was to train soldiers and in turn, I think he viewed my son as someone that needed to be trained that way. He could not turn off the commander part in him anymore. That was just how it was and we had to live with it.

He was extremely hard on my son. If my son did not do what he was told immediately, my husband would explode. Words from his mouth, "Take out the trash" roughly thirty seconds later followed "Why haven't you taken out the trash?" He would then get so angry with my son that I would have to intervene and calm him down. I would explain that he just told him to take out the trash and that it had not been enough time lapsed before he went at him in anger.

His response was always punishment and it never fit the offense. The consequence was never equal to the offense. Everything was big to him. "He didn't take out the trash so no TV for three months." Mistakes made were no longer mistakes to him. My son spilled hot water once and my husband's immediate reaction was to scream "F" this and "F" that to him. It was an accident and he verbally threw the situation into an intense angry encounter. My teenage son came to me bawling in my arms. I found myself now telling my son "we just need to do what he says when he says it," advising him and trying to give him pointers on how to live like this. All the while worrying that my son would tell his father, my ex, and I would lose custody of them. I realized, at this point, I needed to separate his involvement with my children. I collected enough courage and approached him. I told him that he was no longer allowed to discipline them. That everything concerning the children, had to go through me from that point on. I told him that he was not allowed to take anything away from them and that it was all up to me now. We had never had an issue with this prior to deployment. He had always been reasonable. Taking away his ability to discipline the children hurt my relationship with him even more. These were my children though, I needed to protect them and I just could not let that go on. He felt as though I was not backing him up as his wife . . . and I wasn't. He was unreasonable and over demanding. He was changing daily and I needed to protect my children. My thoughts were if I let these verbal assaults continue, then eventually it might escalade to physical encounters and I could not have that.

 I woke daily wondering what that day would bring and wondering what demons he would battle next. Paranoia and defiance were other issues for him. Upon his return from deployment he had gotten involved politically and enjoyed politics now. He became involved in political events locally and studied those he supported. There was an incident at a political rally that he had attended. At the rally, an older woman had a disposable camera in which she used to take his picture. I was not there to witness this myself, but he told me she took his picture and then he took her camera from her. He brought it home and showed it to me. He said, "She took my picture so I took her camera." He said, "She had no right to take my picture." I said, "You did what . . . and they didn't arrest you?" I can only assume from my reaction to what he had done, that he realized perhaps he should not have done that. Prior to my reaction though, I think he felt he was in full authority. He then said he would have the pictures developed and return them to her. He later told me he returned them to her, but I did not know if he had been truthful. The whole incident, it just made me go, "Oh my God."

Arrogance and defiance made life more difficult. Once, while attending a sporting event for my son, they had reserved spaces that we were not allowed to park. He got out of the car and moved the cones and parked there anyway. I begged him to move, but he refused stating that he had fought for the freedom to park anywhere he wanted. He was a soldier. This was a free parking lot, and he could park there if he wanted to. He then said, "Who are they to tell me I can't? They are not the government or the police. They are just part of this event." It was customary to pay to park at these events. He refused. Again he was a soldier who fought for the freedom of this country and who were they to tell him he had to pay to park. During the event, staff approached him and asked him to move his car. He refused. They came up to him again asking him to move and he became combative. They then turned to me. Because of this, the head of the event filed a complaint with the state over his behavior, which almost resulted in my son being kicked out of the athletic association. He had no remorse or consideration for what he had done or how it affected my son and our family. He was defying social rule and doing what he wanted. I was shocked and embarrassed and forced to live like this.

He arrived home in October and by January he had approximately six speeding tickets. In his words "When I'm in the car going down the road, I'm back in Iraq." He actually argued most of those tickets using that statement to the court. He told the judges that in his mindset he is still in Iraq when he is in the car and traveling down the road and in Iraq they could go as fast as they wanted. The judges would say "OK" and he got them dismissed. Granted, before Iraq he did drive fast, but he told me that when we got married, God had told him he needed to slow down. He had a family now and they needed him and he needed to be more careful. When he returned from Iraq, he drove like a bat out of hell. He did not care how fast he was going or who was in the car. Once my parents rode with him from our home to another local city and they said they would never ride with him again. They were terrified. I was constantly scared when riding in the car with him . . . constantly.

When this change in him appeared, I had no clue what was going on. I was an FRG leader, worked with military, and had been around them fifteen to twenty years, yet for months I had no clue what was happening. I finally got to the point where I just got in the car and left. I drove away not knowing where I was going or what I was doing but trying to get away. I was so beside myself. I did not know what to do or who to turn to. In a moment of complete surrender and a humble approach, I reached out to my pastor. He himself had no clue we had been struggling. Everyone at church and in our lives thought everything was fine. My husband had kept up the perfect public appearance. He was an excellent soldier with a perfect Christian family. He needed to be seen this way, with everyone, except with my son and me.

Arguments got worse and the outburst of anger made him unapproachable. He would say horrible things to me, and then an hour later, act like nothing happened or not remember saying them. I do not swear but I would repeat what he had said to me in hopes of shocking him into remembering. I would say, "Do you remember this is what you said to me?" and I would repeat verbatim back to him. He responded, "No, I didn't say that." We would have conversations about bills and finances, and I would follow through with what we had discussed. However, he would get mad at me for following through with our decision. He did not remember our conversation. This would continue three or four times before he actually remembered. He acted like he had never had that conversation all the while being actively involved in it at the time. It was frustrating and frightening to me.

He kept information from me and was secretive. I had noticed on several different occasions that the history on our computer had been erased. This was not just once, but several times that I noticed a complete history gone on the computer. Having a teenage son, I thought perhaps it might have been him. I started observing and logging when the history was erased. Through this I realized it was not my son, but in fact it was my husband who was erasing it. Very frightened and emotionally unprepared for what I was about to approach, I cautiously confronted him. He eventually admitted to me what he had been searching the Internet for . . . *how to build a bomb*. My heart was pounding, my eyes welted up with tears, and my knees felt as though they were going to fail me. I was left speechless. I seriously thought it might have been pornographic material of some sort. With that, I might have been able to reason. I did not know what to say how to respond or what to do. All I knew at that point was that I was scared not only for him but also for others that may encounter him.

Eventually, he started attending school and was not actively involved in the military. He had grown to hate the military. He would state that he hated the army and the military and just wanted to get out and that he wanted nothing to do with the military anymore. He did not want to be deployed anymore, but yet at the same time he would not seek help because it would affect his military career in a negative way. No longer sleeping, he was experiencing flashbacks and nightmares. Confiding in me, only at points of breakdown, he had stated he knew he had PTSD (Post Traumatic Stress Disorder), and that he had all the classic signs of it. He told me he no longer cared if he lived or died. He no longer engaged socially. He struggled with people and group settings like church. He was on a downward spiral. Using these points of contradicting behavior compiled with his anger issues, physical and mental distress, and our struggle as a family, I begged him to get help. There were glimpses of the man I married, but mostly just covered up or a passing glimpse. One of these points, these passing moments that reminded me he still existed, that the man I married was still there, was that he himself was determined to get help. He was going to do what he needed to do to and come back to us. In one of the very few moments that he surrendered to the thought that he may have a problem; he realized this was bigger than him and that he may need to seek out help. He went through Military One Source and received counseling off post. He was OK with this. Of course his counselor said he needed more help than she could offer. She told him he needed medication. He then went back on base to seek the help he knew he needed.

However, he could not get the military to help him. He ended up spending almost two days on post refusing to leave until they assigned him a psychologist. When he finally got help, he was told that he did have PTSD but if they stated that in his records he would not get promoted. If they placed it in his file, his career would be over. By this time he had already submitted a promotion packet and it was received. His PTSD was not listed on it.

He began a program where they relived moments in Iraq in group therapy. It was excruciating not only for him but also for us. He came home angry every day. It was horrible. He said the counselors said it would get worse before it got better, but I never saw "better." What I came to realize was that he felt responsible for the death of that lieutenant and for the burns on that soldier. Because he was the commander that made the decision to go that route, he felt he should have died instead of them and in time he finally admitted that to me. They gave him medication and told him he needed to take it. He took it and did not like it. In order to keep up appearances, he continued to have the prescription filled and stock piled it but never took it. He wanted to make sure that if they looked in his records they would see he was filling the prescription and doing what he was told he needed to do. Remember, keeping up appearances was important to him.

He was on base getting therapy for PTSD but our marriage needed tending to also. I tried to get him to attend counseling with me. We went to our pastor and he only attended three sessions. He refused to go back. He said he felt it was a session just to beat up on him. He was not doing it anymore.

While in therapy for PTSD, there were times when he made a true effort. There were times when I thought that he was recognizing his anger and was able to walk away. Then, I think he just got tired of trying and gave up. Trying became too difficult and it became easier not to make the effort and just to remain in the state he was living in, in a state we were all living in.

We had a situation develop with my son involving my ex, who also made decisions about my son. It was over a gift. My husband felt I had taken my ex's side in the matter and did not speak to me for two weeks. When I finally asked him what was going on, he said, "I'm leaving. I'm not going to stay. I'm not doing this anymore." I said "OK." I did not have work that day so I called a realtor and some friends. By the time he returned home that evening, I had the house lit up and we were painting and cleaning. He called me on his cell from the driveway and asked what was going on. I told him I was getting the house ready to sell. He said, "What do you mean?" I said, "You told me this morning you were leaving and I cannot afford this house on my own." He refused to come in and told me he would be back later. I think at this point I was trying to provoke a reaction from him. Perhaps I was hoping he would see the reality of stating those very powerful words: "I'm leaving. I'm not going to stay. I'm not doing this anymore."

So the house was now up for sale and he approached me one day and said he did not want to be without me. He said he did not want a divorce and he wanted us to try again. I think he felt, at this point, like he was losing and that everyone would know. I submitted and he returned. There was no trying though. It became worse. I do not know why he asked to try again. The effort was never made. We were strangers living in the same house.

He was on his way to a training course and before he left I made my very last effort to save our marriage. I had no doubts he was the man God wanted for me when I married him, and I wanted so much to hold on to him. I asked him if he was going to buy a new house with me. He responded no. I said I love you to him and asked if he loved me. He responded "No, I hate you." I asked him if he was going to stay with me and he responded, "I haven't decided yet." So before he walked out the door to leave, I hit the lowest point of our marriage and fell to my knees. I begged him to stay with me and to forgive me for something I did not even feel I needed to be forgiven for. Loving him? Asking for the man I married? This is what I was begging him to forgive me for? I asked him to come back to me and he just looked at me. He looked at me with no emotion or feeling. I got up off my knees, composed myself and said, "Never again, I am not doing this anymore." He then left and went to his training course. He did not return my calls or text. He talked to me maybe two times in the three months he was gone. So, I moved his things out. He had already told me he was leaving me and that he did not love me and that he was not buying another house with me. With all that said and the way he treated my son . . . I moved his stuff out. I went from trying so hard to love him and bring him back to us, to deciding to do the best I could to take charge of my situation.

He refused to tell me when he was returning home. I would text him and ask, but all I got back was that it was none of my business. He said he would be home when he was home. So I had no idea when he was returning. I lived in fear of not knowing what day he was coming in and fear of his reaction when he realized his belongings were gone.

He returned on a Saturday morning. He walked in and fixed himself something to eat. He sat down, watched TV, and never said a word to me. I finally called him to our bedroom and told him that I thought we needed to talk. He said, "OK, what?" I asked him if he was ready to buy a house with me, and he said no. I asked him if he was ready to attend counseling with me, and he said no. I asked if he wanted to stay married to me, and he said he did not know. At that point, I told him that I had moved his things into storage and that he no longer lived here. He looked at me and said, "OK, I'm going upstairs to take a nap." Four hours later, he came downstairs, and I told him we needed to get out of the house, that it had a realtor showing. Our beautiful dream home, sold that day. That night when he realized he had no place to go, he called me over and over again on my cell screaming, yelling and angry. I told him, "I'm sorry you are not staying here. You cannot treat me like this and continue to live with me." Soon after, he filed for divorce. I would have never filed. Just because we could not live together did not mean I had given up. I was still praying for a miracle. I wanted that man God gave me in the beginning. I wanted that godly man that cared for and loved us so very much.

We were divorced and a couple of months later he sent me a letter. It was typed, not handwritten, stating that he was sorry for everything he had done knowing it was his anger and PTSD that had driven us apart. Of course, I was still angry and hurt, so I texted him a message stating that he knew where I lived and knew my address and phone number. I asked him, "What part of having a five-year marriage makes you think that a typed letter is an acceptable apology?" He agreed with what I had said and asked to meet me at a local coffee shop. He sat across the table from me, with sincere expression and apologized. He said he had no idea why God saved him and why he had not died over there. He told me he felt as though he had nothing left. He spoke of a conversation he had with the parents of his former lieutenant and how he had asked them to forgive him for killing their child. After obtaining their forgiveness, he stated he finally felt like he could start living again. I honestly think he had certain expectations as a Christian man going to war. I felt that he expected no one to die under his command. He prayed for those soldiers prior to deployment. We both had prayed for those soldiers. Having lost those under his command made him question God and His existence.

He informed me he was getting counseling, but for me, it was too late. After that meeting with him, I was confused as to what to do so I spoke with my pastor again. He very bluntly said to me that the man I married died over there. He said you are divorced and you need to live your life. God wants you to live.

I felt jealousy of some sort. I had a friend that lost her husband in a helicopter crash and she became a widow. She received benefits from the military, and she had a different stigma than I did. I felt like I lost my husband to this war just as she had. I felt like I was a victim and that I deserved the same amount of consideration that they had given her . . . yet all I received was a divorce.

When he left, it was a relief to my children. They do not talk about him. They do not ask about him and they do not miss him. They saw it all: all the fights, arguments, and anger; that was all they remembered.

There were times when I wished he had died over there instead of coming back. There were a lot of moments when I wished that he had never made it back to us. Maybe if he had died, I could still have loved him. I could have loved that man God had blessed me with and honored him as a loving husband, stepfather, and soldier.

I blamed the army for his emotional and mental disappearance. I believe the army turned a blind eye; unless the soldier had a visible injury, they were not considered injured. I think the military tried to hide the suicide rate among soldiers and the effect it had on the spouses and children of these returning soldiers. In the end, there were soldiers that walked away without help or benefits because they had been trained not to report what hurt, trained not to get profiles, and trained not to record it. In turn, they trained their spouses not to seek help and to cover up what emotional and mental distress they may have been living with.

The Price of Silence

Dating exclusively, at the young age of sixteen, does not always work out for the young couple. It can evolve into an emotional and hormonal circus that more or less ends in heartache. Then again, it can be the start of a life with the one person that knows you better and loves you more than anyone else.

I dated my husband throughout most of our high school years. After high school, I took a job in an investment firm and he attended junior college. My husband worked part time for an aircraft engine company and started flight lessons on weekends. Flying soon became a life goal for him, and I was determined to help him achieve that goal.

We married at the very young age of twenty. A year later with savings and a loan from his parents, he was enrolled in a civilian flight school. We quit our jobs and we were on our way to pursue his dream of flying and one day, flying for a living.

We rented a small one-bedroom apartment, and life consisted of nonstop studying and school. I was by his side helping him to obtain his civilian licenses . . . all of them. Every certification the school offered, he obtained. He did all this in a very short span of one year. He always pursued with a hundred-percent-type attitude. He was determined to pass these courses and become a pilot. He did, and he did so at the top of his class.

Upon completion of flight school, jobs were scarce and hard to find. He took a job with a parcel service but was frustrated and unhappy. Still applying nationwide, he became intolerant of his unsuccessful attempts to obtain a flight job. At this point, he would accept or do anything to fly and I wanted this for him. This passion for flying soon took us down a life road I never could have imagined.

My husband started looking into opportunities to fly helicopters in the US Army. After going through the whole recruiting process from start to finish, he was denied flight school due to his allergies as a child. His recruiter had convinced him that if he entered the army, it would be easier to obtain flight school from the inside rather than a civilian from the outside. Once he was in service, they would pick him over someone on the outside. He neglected to tell him that being denied medically because of allergies would never be reconsidered. My husband pursuing his flying career listened to this recruiter and joined the US Army.

Now in the army, he held the position as a crew chief. However, his job was to maintain the aircraft, not to fly it. He was part of the enlisted community and working hard toward flying an aircraft he came to know very well. He was admired by the officers/pilots because of his flight knowledge and often consulted on how to fly certain areas cross-country and really in any field of flying he could help them with. He was a fixed wing pilot; they were rotary wing pilots. Each wanted what the other had. He was not just any enlisted soldier; he was admired and treated well by the officer community to the point where you would never know he was not an officer himself.

Holding his fixed wing ratings, he took a job on weekends, flying skydivers to earn extra money and to keep a "current" flight status.

With one vehicle, I was home by myself most of the time. I did not mind it at the time because this was important to him, and he was working toward a life goal that would benefit us both. Still grateful for my partnership, he had spoken often of how blessed he was to have me by his side.

Making several attempts at being accepted into Warrant Officer Candidate (WOC) school just seemed to be a waste of time. Each packet that was sent off returned with the same denial. They would not take him because of his allergies as a child. Officers/pilots wrote letters for him and tried their best to get him accepted on their own merit. Still a denial came back every time. It was hard to watch his disappointment each time, and I was struggling to understand why the army would not take such a great prospect. I knew, knowing him, he would actually be the best in this field or at least one of the top prospects. I would later learn that I was not wrong about that.

We were stationed stateside for three years, and then assigned an overseas tour in Germany. We were living in Germany, plus one child, and on our last attempt to get the army to accept him into flight school. The army gives you five chances and this was our last shot at it. He had pretty much given up. He was not seeing any other way of getting accepted. His new plan was to go green to gold, to become an officer. With this option, hopefully, somehow, he could manage to at least work in the aviation field. He was discouraged, but I was on a mission to help my husband obtain his dream of flying and I did just that.

After some research on my own and copies of his resume, I composed letters to a few senators. I explained his situation stating that he was a civilian pilot and his inability to gain acceptance into the army's flight program due to allergies as a child. I was successful! I received a letter back from a senator explaining how to obtain a medical waver, a waver that no one had ever mentioned to us before. The senator included a letter of recommendation for my husband and a personal letter of well wishes and admiration for his continuing efforts to serve in the aviation field of the US Army. I was so happy about this. My husband had hope again and it was because of my efforts. I was so proud of myself for pursuing this, not letting him give up and taking the steps to do this for him. A few months later, he was accepted into the US Army's flight program. He was very excited and I was extremely happy for him . . . really happy for us.

Alabama was home to flight school for the army. Soldiers, while attending, could have their families with them. It was a great set up for us. We lived on base and among others attending flight school. Time together was abundant, and it could not have worked out better. With the arrival of our second child, bonding as a family of four was easily done there.

When the kids were younger, my husband was a very active dad. At night, I had time to work out while he fed them and had gotten bath time over and done with. A few less things I had to do at night, and he was thrilled to spend the time with them. He was kind of amazing and I bragged about him often. He knew how stressful raising kids could be and always told me I did it well. He was always extremely supportive and encouraging. I appreciated his ability to listen and support me. He always had though. Even as dating teenagers, he was my best friend, playmate, and huge support. I knew back then he would one day turn out to be a great husband and wonderful dad. I was right.

After flight school we were given orders to another stateside duty station. This was a great move for us. His career as a military pilot was taking off and he had obtained "Top Gun" status while stationed there. He was new to the military's pilot world, so this was a huge feat for him. I was a very proud wife. We lived on base and hardly owned anything but we sure had fun. I remember times when the kids and I would wait just inside the front glass storm door. We would stand there waiting for him to arrive home. He knew if all three of us were at the door, dinner was going to be on him that night. He would pull up into the driveway, smile that huge smile he had upon seeing us, and we would all run to his truck. He knew how to play with us and how to make us smile. There were times when I would call him at work, leave embarrassing messages for him and the other pilots would post them on the public dry erase board. I remember when he would have me paged, at the grocery store, for no good reason at all and I would find myself midaisle, laughing. That was just stuff we did . . . others saw it and slightly envied the relationship. I was an encouragement to him just as he was to me. We were playmates; the very best of friends and loving him was easy.

His unit received orders to Bosnia for an eight-month rotation. Things had started to get stressful now gearing up for his first big deployment. He was excited. He referred to it as their "Super Bowl." It was something they trained and practiced so hard for. He needed to talk about the day and training and I was there to listen. I listened, asked questions, and participated in conversation just because I knew he needed me to be there for him. Honestly, I mostly never understood much of anything he said. Military boys talk in code . . . even to their wives. I spent many years learning the military lingo/code and had gotten pretty good at it. I had listened, supported, and been everything he needed me to be, just as he had always been for me.

The Bosnia deployment was upon us. He returned home from work one evening and said he had to leave on the advanced party to Bosnia. I really did not know what that meant at the time but I did know he was leaving before everyone else. I did ask, why him? His response was that he volunteered to go. At first I was shocked, but "shocked" passed quickly and I was livid. I asked why he would do such a thing. "Why would you choose to be away from us two extra weeks?" His response was that they were going to pick him anyway. I was so hurt and angry . . . I responded, "I would have let them pick me." So for two weeks, I watched as the other wives spent time with their husbands before they deployed. I watched knowing mine volunteered to leave us early. He never saw it that way. He saw it as an opportunity to look good to the command . . . and he took it. Being the person I was and knowing me as well as he did, he knew I would never confront the command or ask questions as to why my husband went first and others stayed behind. I did what I was expected to do and kept to myself.

The unit had returned home after eight months and life resumed as normal. About a year later (maybe less), he received orders to Korea with a return duty station back to the first base we were ever assigned. We were excited about this move. It was our first duty station and we had good memories of our time there. We made the decision that we would build a house this time, and the kids and I would move in just before he left for Korea.

The move was not easy. We had been in the process of building a house and it was not finished. My husband had orders to Korea and decided, on his own, to take an unnecessary course prior to his Korea assignment. He had just added three more months of unnecessary time away from us by doing this. His justification was that he did not want to be the "Bitch boy" while in Korea. I guess his plan failed. Several phone calls to me while in Korea he stated he was just the "Bitch boy." I did not get it, but again I kept my mouth shut and did what I was supposed to do.

While my husband was serving his time in Korea, I was alone in a new state knowing all of about two people. Anything I did was on my own and brand-new . . . but I was doing it. I would send care packages to him and wait by the computer for his video call. I made sure to remind the kids that their daddy loved them and that he wished he could have been there with us. I always reassured them and myself that he missed us and could not wait to be with us again. This was what my days consisted of.

I was probably about a month into him being gone that I became ill. I woke one morning off balance. I felt as though I was falling to my left. Trips to the doctor were unsuccessful in diagnosing my condition. I was referred to an ENT and he put me through a few standard office tests. He ordered a CT scan and MRI. As I was leaving his office, he said it was a probably an ear tumor or brain tumor. Seriously? Why would he have said that to a patient not knowing for sure? So now I am in a thirty-day wait for an MRI and CT scan thinking I'm slowly dying. I was still functioning as sole caregiver to my children, and my condition was slowly becoming worse.

I was in daily contact with my husband keeping him informed of my condition. Waiting by the computer in hopes of hearing from him is what I did daily. I needed him. I was alone and dealing with a condition that I had been told was probably deadly. I recall one day talking to him and telling him I did not sleep at night. I told him I sometimes needed to hear him and talk to him. Armed with the knowledge that he had a phone in his room, I then asked if I could have his phone number. His response was paused and then he said, "No, I don't want you to bother me." I did not react right away to his response; instead I tried to process why my husband would have said this to me. He had known my condition and that I had been unbelievably stressed. He knew that an incompetent doctor told me that I could possibly have some type of tumor, yet he had responded to my request in a selfish and self-centered way . . . one that was almost inconceivable. It was a selfish and hurtful response. To this day, I still hurt when I think about it or speak of it. A stranger, knowing what I was going through, would never have said that to me. My husband of over ten years did. He did not want me to bother him. At this point I wondered if his career and position in the service had made its way as a more valuable factor than his wife's physical condition.

Still dealing with being off balance, I now had physical pain and an inability to stand without my legs giving out upon first try. I had ear pain and half my face was numb. I called on my parents to come and their arrival was quick upon my request. They stayed with me for a month and during this time I had the MRI and CT scan. They were a support and helped to lessen my stress. The ENT read my CT and MRI and told me there was nothing wrong with me. He told me from what I had described to him I was stressed. I am betting by this point he was right. I am sure to this day, it started with him telling me thirty days prior that I probably had ear or brain tumors.

I was cleared by the ENT and just left to figure it out on my own. I told my husband I needed help finding out what was going on with me. He took his permitted leave and returned home. He was able, through a friend, to have me seen by an allergist without a referral. Upon calling up my MRI and CT, scan the allergist told me I had a massive sinus infection that had invaded me for over six months. The ENT had missed it. Through sinus surgery and medication, I recovered.

With everything I went through, the vertigo, physical symptoms, and stress of thinking I was dying, the most vivid memory of that time was still my husband denying me his phone number. The reason he gave me has stayed with me to this day . . . he did not want to be bothered by me. We did discuss it when he returned home from Korea. He said they had lost a crew in an accident over there. He said the command encouraged them not to let problems back home distract them from the mission. My husband had taken this to heart, pushed me aside, and focused on his job in Korea. He responded later, not with an apology but with an excuse as to why he said that, and I quote "Yeah, that was probably not one of my high points." He never apologized but it is a piece of my heart that was torn . . . torn by him.

He returned home from Korea but not before he yet again took another course to further his career. That twelve months to Korea turned into eighteen months with all of the courses he added before and after. I never shared with anyone that he took those courses and did not need to. To me it was embarrassing that he chose to do that. I look back and see it now as a very selfish decision he had made. I told others that they made him do it, that it was part of his assignment to Korea . . . and he let me.

After eighteen months he returned home. Things were great at first as they usually were when he first returned. Slowly though, things began to go downhill. I remember screaming it out in the kitchen one day telling him that I hated living like this. The fights, although never in front of the kids, were not normal for us. We did not fight. We did now. The majority of our disagreements were because of me. I was always battling for his time. I wanted him to come home for dinner, go to lunch with me, and spend time with us. It was not going to happen though. I was a military wife and we had to learn to deal with what we were dealt. We did not interfere with the career or mission in anyway shape or form. It would look bad on the soldier and prevent him from furthering his military career . . . so he said.

Upon his return, he had been temporally assigned to a stationary unit on base because the new unit he was assigned to still had not yet returned from Iraq. He poured tons of time and extra time into his temporary assignment in hopes of getting assigned to them later in his career. I was naive and believed what he told me when it came to his work. I was told this could set us up for no more deployments in the future. Little did I know (and found out a year later) that the job went on seniority and time served. There were so many ahead of him, he would not have obtained that job till retirement. So I smiled and watched as he volunteered his services and extra family time for nothing. It was not for nothing though. He was admired, told "thank you" repeatedly, and considered to be exactly what any commander had ever hoped for. He was a soldier pouring 110 percent into his job and at times doing the jobs of others. If he was asked to, volunteered or ordered to, the outcome was the same. He would go above and beyond and left huge impressions. He was exactly what I knew he would be in the beginning. He was top in his field and the best of the best. He knew this and it was very important to him.

He was working for the unit that had just returned from Iraq. This was good. With their return, it would keep him stateside for a while. Things were getting better, and it was life as our "normal." Our children were involved in league sports and he was showing up to games, practices, and even picking them up from school when he could. He was their hero, buddy, and one big playmate. They loved their daddy. He would pull up into the driveway and they would race to see who could get to him first. I knew it was because he was gone a lot and I played my part in "beefing" him up to be the best dad ever. I would tell them things like "our country is grateful to daddy for doing what he does." I never ever had them think otherwise of him. That was their daddy. They loved the time with him and craved it. Never in a million years did I ever think that would change.

For the next year it was pretty much routine. His unit was training to go back to Iraq and this time he would be with them. This would be his first rotation to Iraq. He worked a lot preparing to deploy. Training was the priority and I supported that and understood. I accepted him telling me he had to work, would not be home till late, and could not take a day off. They were training. That is all we heard about. It became normal to the kids and I that we ate dinner without him. Sundays were great because he was home and after church we would go out to dinner or grill out by the pool. It was really the only day we were allotted.

His deployment date grew closer and I was trying my best to include him in as much as possible so that he did not miss out. They were deploying just before Thanksgiving and I came up with the plan that we would have "Turkey Day" a week before Thanksgiving. It was fun. We decorated; I invited my friend over and made an awesome Thanksgiving feast. Honestly, it felt just like Thanksgiving Day. The kids loved it and I loved that he was not going to miss out. We were "thankful" that day.

That deployment was a rough one. They lost six pilots in the first three months they were over there. I believe this was not just in Iraq but other pilots they knew serving in other parts of the world were lost in this timeframe. At the time of an incident, they cut communication from soldiers to families until the family members are notified. There were times when it was twenty-four hours or so until we would hear who went down and if it was our spouse or not. It was so mentally taxing that I felt it physically. When I would see him again, via computer, or hear his voice, I was overwhelmed. It is an indescribable feeling hearing he was alive and well, yet mourning and hurting for the family who had just suffered a lost. I knew what we as spouses went through over here. I could not imagine still having to function as a soldier, in time of war, after losing a coworker and friend . . . a brother, as they became to each other.

My husband was good about computer chatting. I waited by the computer often never knowing when he was going to be there. My life became an unending wait. In between waiting for communication from him I raised my children. I felt like I was just going through the motions until he came home and then we would resume our lives together as a family. His time computer chatting was spent asking about me, the kids, and life back home. He never mentioned the mission or what was happening there. It was just all about us. He wanted to know everything and could not express enough how much he missed us and loved us.

His R&R (Rest and Relaxation) was assigned and he came home for two weeks. That is exactly where we stayed . . . home. We played in the pool, grilled, and just hung out for two weeks together as a family. He was happy and thrilled to be home and back with us. You could see he was trying to get as much of us as he could before he had to return . . . back to that war zone. The place that now held horrid memories of brothers lost and now a fear of what else may come. He went back to finish his deployment and the kids and I went back to waiting. Waiting for his next letter, video chat, and ultimately his return home.

As time passed slowly and his return grew closer, the excitement built within me. I passed this on to my children by speaking of his return home and how it was growing closer. Never did I have a definite date. That really was not ever set in stone. We had a rough estimate. Preparing for daddy to return was a huge deal. I made sure it was. We made a sign to have at his homecoming. I purchased a welcome home banner, balloons, a cake . . . the works. I had a friend come to take pictures of the reunion. We were ready. I remember it like it was yesterday. Standing on my feet in the stands of a gym on base, my son holding his "Welcome Home, Daddy" sign and my daughter holding balloons. Families were screaming with excitement as those soldiers filed through that gym door. They had lined the soldiers up on the floor in front of us and I could hear nothing. The nonstop screaming coming from the stands was overwhelming. At this point I was focused on looking for my husband and was looking through tear-filled eyes. I found him! He had the biggest smile of anyone and was easy to spot. I pointed him out to the kids as I began to cry, uncontrollably. As soon as they dismissed the soldiers, a wave of people rolled from the stands to the gym floor. All were looking frantically to find their soldier and welcome them home. I held onto my children and waited for the opportunity myself to enter the floor and run to him. That was exactly what we did. We ran to him. We were so relieved to have him home and back with us and so overwhelmed by the return home ceremony and atmosphere of absolute joy. My husband held onto all three of us like he never wanted to let go. I was grateful to have him back yet sadden by the families that lost during that deployment. It is a feeling you tend to struggle with inside. If I was feeling that, I can not imagine what the returning soldier felt like; having left in formation with these men and returning in formation without them. Their families not there to welcome them home but still the vision of them there waving goodbye. Never would I wish that on anyone. Sadly, that was part of being a soldier in today's world.

The first two weeks of his return home were fun and exciting. We spent a lot of time together and getting back into the swing of being a complete family again. It was about a month after his return home that I noticed slight changes in him. People annoyed him. He was easily angered especially when talking about work. He would come home and discuss his day with me and his demeanor, voice, and actions were that of an angry person. I remember telling the kids that mommy and daddy were not fighting but that daddy was just telling me something about work. He had gotten so worked up that the children assumed we were fighting. I reminded him often that he was speaking to me, his wife, not those who have angered him. He would then back off and finish what he was saying in a calmer manner. I just assumed he was getting use to work again like home and that his anger would subside. I did not realize at the time, that this was the beginning and there was more to come.

As a couple we started to battle again. It was always work stuff really. I wanted him home to spend time and to help out but he wanted to be at work. He never stated he wanted to be at work but he was always the first one there and the last one to leave. He volunteered a lot filling in and doing stuff for other pilots. All the while, he would tell me he had to do it. I only know he volunteered because other wives would tell me. Stating that my husband was great for taking their husbands spot on a flight or static display weekend. He always denied it. He would just tell me that it was his turn in the rotation.

A few months passed and he was still exhausting his time and effort into work. Claiming he hated it yet only knowing how to function within it. I listened to him vent daily and tried to figure out why he had such anger . . . praying that it would soon subside. His emotional state had become questionable and tears were shed for things others and I did not deem tear worthy. I often wondered if that was all just part of his anger. Perhaps it was just being released in an alternate emotional way. I never understood it and at times the crying would actually annoy me. Outburst and struggling to even communicate became more of an issue.

    I woke one morning and went into the kitchen. He was there watching TV and drinking coffee. I did not say anything at that moment but noticed his wedding ring was missing. He had never been without that ring. When married, I placed it on his hand; he wore it and never took it off. A few days later I recall looking specifically for it on his hand. It was still missing. I had to ask. I asked him why he was not wearing it. He told me he was up and down off that aircraft every day and did not want to get it hung up on something. He said there was a poster at work showing detail of how a ring could get caught and cause damage to your finger or hand. He said he was afraid of it getting ripped off his hand. I know what poster he was talking about but it had been up and posted way before he decided to take his ring off. I was not buying his answer anyway. You see, years earlier, when he was a crew chief on the aircraft he now piloted, he did get that ring caught up on the aircraft and it was ripped off his finger. He had to have the ring fixed. As soon as it was, he placed it back on his hand and did not remove it . . . at least not until now. So his excuse, as to why he was not wearing the ring, never made sense. I waited a few months and at breakfast one morning my son noticed he had no wedding ring on. When my son asked why he was not wearing it, my husband gave him the same "poster at work" story he gave me. I just listened but still did not accept this as the truth. Later, my husband was on the porch sitting, looking down, and messing with some gadget that he was trying to fix. I walked out to the porch and again asked the same question. I said, "Really, why are you not wearing your ring?" He looked up at me, in a moment I will never forget, with his eyes only . . . it was a frightening look . . . it was cold and full of hate. He never answered me; he just looked back down at what he was doing. I walked back into the house and swore to myself that I would never ask him about it again. I was hurt, devastated, and slightly scared. It was roughly six months later that I noticed his wedding ring was on his dog tags around his neck. I did not acknowledge it. A few more months passed and his wedding ring was back on his hand. I never got an answer as to why he took it off for a year. If indeed he was worried about it getting ripped off his hand, what changed? He was still a pilot; he was still up and down off the aircraft daily. Why put it back on? It did not make sense to me. That was another thing I never told anyone about. I kept that to myself. It was embarrassing and hurtful and if I told anyone, it would make him look bad and looking bad to others was never going to happen.

I noticed things he enjoyed before had become a distraction to him and ended up getting pushed aside. He loved our yard and working in it. When he returned from his deployment, he no longer enjoyed it. My son and I would mow and all he would have to do is edging. He could not even do that without complaining. He looked at the pool, the yard, and our house as more work and he no longer wanted to do it or had time for it. He was too busy going to work early and staying late. Any request I made was quickly dismissed with an excuse as to why we could not do that. It had gotten to the point that if anything needed to be fixed I took it upon myself to do it and stopped asking him.

Before he started deployment he would move mountains for me. If I needed something done he was there to do it. I was always grateful and he was happy that his efforts thrilled me as they did. We did not have money and I was not one to demand items as a show of affection. I was more of a please-fix-that-for-me kind of girl. So if the sink needed fixing, I was thrilled that he did that for me. After Iraq, it was not enough. I noticed his efforts went to those outside our family. The people at work, neighbor's, people at church, these were now the ones his efforts went toward. He was not only the returning hero to others but his contributions to them made him "God like" in their eyes. He liked that. I played my part in this. I never spoke badly about him and I always told others of his greatness not only as a husband but also as a father. He too spoke highly of us. People stopped me, at times, and said that all he talked about was the kids and I and how blessed he was. All this was for him though; we made him look good too.

Throughout that year, they were again training to go back to Iraq. When they were training to go the first time, I just accepted it. This time I kind of fought it. I knew he would be gone for a year again and I wanted him home for dinner, kids' ballgames, and Saturdays. Yes, they took a few of those from us too.

Work became his main priority and I was told only what he wanted me to know. I was never one of those wives that showed up at their husbands work or hung out and waited for them to be released. I looked at it as something that would embarrass him and I myself looked down on those women that hung out at the hanger or offices. Sadly, the distance I was keeping from his work was being used against me. It was not until years later, at his retirement ceremony, that my suspicions were confirmed. A commander thanked him for volunteering for weekend duties and extra missions so others did not have to. He still walked out of there denying it to me. I guess now, what I looked at as respect and trust for my husband was actually an enabling factor.

He was pouring himself into work and I continued to be the waiting military wife. Always supporting him telling others how great he was and never leading on how slowly the man I married was disappearing before my eyes. He was turning into a self-centered angry man with little regard for his family, a family he longed to be with while deployed and one he desperately had missed.

My husband was training constantly and mainly irritated, stressed, and quick to anger. I suggested a few times that perhaps he might need to talk to someone. Mainly, just to get the last Iraq off his chest. He said no. I recall after the arrest of one of his former commanders, we had a long talk about Iraq and his commander. I told him if he did not get help that he was going to end up just like him. I started crying as I pleaded with him to go talk to someone. I sat crying on my bathroom floor and slowly looked up at him. He walked over to me, picked me up off the floor and said, *"Absolutely not."* Right then, right there, I realized this is how I was going to have to live. I could tell no one that he was struggling and he was not getting help.

Deployment number two to Iraq happened and again with the horrid goodbyes. We were there at 5:30 a.m. in a parking lot on base saying goodbye for yet another year. The kids were older and wiser as to what he did over there and the danger involved in it. It was very emotional with a lot of uncontrollable crying. I felt emotional for the pain that my children were feeling during their goodbye, but not because he was leaving. I did not really understand why I felt that way. I loved this man, he was about to go fight a war and yet I have no emotions one way or another about him leaving. Another "moment" I kept to myself.

That year the kids and I became very close. They were getting older now and I could stop being so strict. Our time together was fun. We worked out together, played together, and they helped to maintain our home. My son and I took on the yard work and our yard looked amazing. I was so proud of my son and how he stepped up when his dad left. He helped me fix a dishwasher and took care of the daily maintenance on our pool. Anything else that went wrong, he was right there to help with the repair. It was really nice having the kids older during this deployment.

Time with my husband on the computer was almost identical to his last deployment. He wanted to know everything about our day. He could not get enough. It was actually better communication than when he was home. He scheduled R&R for Christmas and it worked out perfectly. The kids were out of school and he had the whole two weeks with us. We had an amazing time together and I would proclaim it as one of our best Christmases ever.

I continued the second half of the deployment as I approached the first half: Working out, hanging out with the kids, and just taking on projects to stay busy. Life while they are deployed seems like one big "wait."

His return home was approaching quickly and we started to prepare again with balloons, banner, and cake. His return home ceremony was held on a parade field on base this time. After a short speech by the commander, they were released to find their families. It took us awhile but we found him. He was in shock at the sight of the kids. They had grown so much since he left. They were kids when he left and teens when he returned.

For the first three months things at home were good. We were getting back into the swing of things and living as a family of four again. However, it was not long I noticed anger appearing in him again. Sometimes his rage was out of nowhere. He was annoyed with people at work and with us. We as a couple had a few arguments where I had asked him if we could seek counseling. He said no. I told him I thought he needed to speak to a counselor. He again said no.

I told him he was different, angry, and needed to talk to somebody. He said no and that there was nothing wrong with him.

Throughout the months, his anger elevated and he had been the hardest on my son. When my husband would ask my son to perform some task or chore, my son would procrastinate. Without warning, my husband would jump immediately to a heightened level of anger. When I would defend my son, he told me that our son was lazy and did nothing. I laughed! I said, "He has done it all, for a year, while you were gone . . . you just weren't here to see it. He was pulling *A*s and *B*s, played sports, and still took care of the yard, pool, and anything else I needed him to do." I stated to him that upon his return home, our son saw him as an extra person to help out and he could back off some. I told him now that he was home, our son was most likely hoping for a break. I stated to him that all he chose to see was a lazy teenager. My husband never wanted to "ease back into family life and day-to-day duties at home." That was printed in some reintegration paperwork we were given to help them adjust to coming back home. He wanted us to continue to do what we did while he was deployed and his focus would be work. Work was never an issue for him. If he needed to work straight through the night to complete or accomplish something there, he would. Stressed-out as he seemed about work, it was a comfort to him. He was happy there. Home soon became uncomfortable to him, as did we.

His demeanor and emotions had changed. I started to notice he rarely smiled anymore. If you knew him, you knew that man always smiled. People use to say that was how they could pick him out of a crowd. Sadly this had disappeared. Most of our family activities evolved around what he liked to do. I have to admit I did this. I made it my goal to try to snap him out of this. If it meant pushing myself aside and doing things that he liked in hopes of seeing him happy,

I was all for it. Camping, fishing, and watching the kids play ball soon became all we did. It was not enough though. He still was not happy. Life for him became more stressful and he was now taking it out on us.

Our fights and disagreements usually had begun with him asking me "What's wrong?" I would respond with my days stress and things that went wrong in hopes of him listening, just as he use to. Instead I received anger, yelling, and a turn of focus from me to him. This was odd to me and it happened often. He would raise his voice to me and ask me what the hell I wanted him to do about it. He would start shouting that he was working his ass off all day long and having to come home to this crap here that needed to be done . . . he shouted "It never stops!" So I listened to him shout it out about work, the command, and his stress. I would then apologize to him. I would begin making things OK for him. I would do this by telling him it was going to get better and that I was there for him. I was always making life better for him or at least I was trying to. This became a way of life for me and soon I realized I had no one to talk to anymore, certainly not him, certainly not my friends or family, and certainly not anyone that could help him. I was lying to everyone and portrayed him as the perfect soldier, husband, and father . . . and he let me; maybe not exactly let me but probably believed himself that he was. I was emotionally alone and protecting him at the cost of my own well-being.

My husband was working for a new unit and traveling the world at times to train others in his aircraft. In the past, the kids and I hated when he had to leave and really missed him when he was gone. We were thrilled to see him return. It was different now. "Do you have to go?" changed to "When are you leaving again?" I noticed the kids and I felt better with him gone. We were more relaxed and we laughed more.

My children and I were always close. It had always just been the three of us and my husband came and went. When he was gone, it was the three of us, and when he would come home; it was still just the three of us. He would eat dinner with us, help clean up, and then disappear into another room. That is where he would stay until he fell asleep. I did ask him why he leaves the room and why he did not stay with us. His response was "I can't stand the shows you guys watch." He was very uncomfortable in our family setting. It was as if he were living in a stranger's home and not his own. He was not interested in hanging out with crowds or going to company events. He was uncomfortable when we would have people over to the house. He was changing fast and I could not stop it. His attitude toward everyone changed, including the children and me.

In the past, before deployments, he made an effort with me. As his wife I did a really good job maintaining myself for him and he always let me know how great I looked or appreciated my efforts to keep in shape. That all went away. I still busted my hump but never received complements from him again. The words "I love you" became a general statement to all of us as he flew out the door on his way to work. I asked him once why he never told me he loved me anymore. He responded, "You know I love you" and walked away. I told him that it would be nice to hear again. He did not respond. The more I pushed the further away he became. His comments to me became passive aggressively mean. I felt emotionally cut off by him and he verbally hit me hard.

When we were younger his mother wore a perfume that he could not stand. He would sneeze, his eyes would water, and he would have attacks at the first smell of it. We would privately tease each other about his mother's fragrance. I approached him one day, after purchasing a new perfume and asked if he liked it. He told me no and that I smelled like his mother. I guess I tell this because it was a deliberate hit to me. It was a turning point for me and I no longer felt he wanted me as a wife. I was already being neglected emotionally and now he was lashing out at my expense.

My husband seemed to say the right things to everyone, sometimes even to the kids and I, but his actions were so opposite. It was as if he knew what he was supposed to be doing and feeling but did not have it in him to connect. The kids asked me in conversation one day, "Why does Daddy fake laugh?" I told them I think your dad knows he is supposed to be laughing so he fakes laugh as not to draw attention. I knew exactly what they were talking about when they had asked me that question. I had myself observed him delayed in reaction and "faking a laugh."

Confrontations were now frequent and not just with me. His reaction to people in public who he felt were doing him wrong was anything but passive. His confrontations with our son became more frequent and more intense. I remember telling my son in private not to defy him and to do exactly what he says and not to argue any point with him. I told him if he would do this, that any issue he may have with what he was told, I would handle it. I do not know why I felt the need to tell my son this but I know now that there was a fear I buried within me but naturally my maternal being stepped up. Walking on eggshells around him, never rocking the boat, always giving him first choice, and his way in everything . . . my feelings, wants . . . they no longer mattered. I started resenting the fact that I no longer had the fun, loving, and kind husband I once knew. I loved this man with all of my mind, body and soul. A love that was so deep that I physically ached when we were apart. Now this same man, I feared.

I told no one in fear of destroying his career. He emphasized how important it was not to do or say anything that may taint his career. I stayed silent. No one knew not even my parents. He thought he was the perfect soldier, perfect husband, and perfect dad; I told him and everyone else that he was.

I know at this point that my husband had a problem, refused to get help and we all had to live with it. I was giving 100 percent and getting nothing back. He became robotic. He went through life's motions without feeling. The more I questioned him, the more defensive he became. So I stopped. Now I am stuck in a marriage walking on eggshells daily, with no one to talk to and loneliness setting in.

Moments of outburst became more frequent. I remember standing in the kitchen one morning having a quiet conversation with him that turned suddenly into a one-sided outburst. The words he used were not even subject related and he went way off topic. It was actually a pleasant conversation until he started yelling. All of it witnessed by my son who was left wondering what just happened. Of course I apologized quickly and told him that I was sorry if I said anything to upset him and if he took it wrong. Again, making everything better. I had begun to tire from making amends constantly. That afternoon when I picked my son up from school he said, "What was Daddy talking about this morning?" I told him I had no clue. Then he said to me, "Mama, I know you don't have anyone to talk to anymore but you'll always have me." Even he could see I was being shut out and the strain it was on me emotionally. I responded with held back tears and a simple "Thank you." This was one of many odd outburst or fits we witnessed from my husband, none of them ever making sense or fitting the situation at hand. This is how we lived.

I was going along day by day at this point wondering how to get him to realize he needed help and at least speak with someone about it. He still refused. If he sought help, he felt he would look weak to his command. On a good day he would admit something was not right with him. On a bad day he stated that he was fine and I was messed up for even suggesting otherwise. However, I was not the one losing control and letting anger rule my being.

One evening my son had lost his class ring. He was franticly looking for it. In our family room there was a picture table and a drawer in this table. It was a "junk" drawer. Nothing in this drawer made any sense. It contained batteries; phone accessories, pens, tape, flyers . . . your typical "junk" drawer. Most people have one. As my daughter and I lay in my bed watching TV, my son continued to look for his ring. He had walked out the garage door to search his truck again. Down the hall in the back of the house, my husband appeared in our bedroom doorway. His words were "I am going to go off on your son." I looked at him with disbelief and calmly asked "Why?" He said that he had destroyed the drawer and left it a mess. With an inner sigh of relief I said, "Oh, well just tell him to clean it up and put it back." I thought my son had dumped it and left. My husband said nothing. He turned and walked back down the hall and into the kitchen. My son came back into the house and that is when it all began. He started yelling at my son. It was unwarranted and made no sense at all. I could hear this from the bedroom and my room was on the other end of the house. His voice was so elevated and evil telling my son he was good for nothing and lazy and that he cared about no one but himself. I then heard a plea that haunts me to this day, my son begging my husband to please tell him what he did wrong. At that moment my daughter said to me, "Mama, go!" I took off down the hall and upon arriving in the kitchen I saw my husband with his fist clinched and veins popping, my son backed up against the kitchen counter begging his father to tell him what he did wrong. I slowly stepped in-between them and sent my son to his room. I looked over toward the drawer. There was nothing wrong with it. I asked him to please tell me what he did to the drawer. My husband's response was "I had a pile of business cards in the corner of that drawer and he moved them around." I knew this was not right and his state of mind was in question. I began talking to him as though he were a three-year-old in order to calm him down. I said that I was sorry, that I did not know this was his drawer and that we would make it his. I pulled the drawer out, removed anything that was not his, and stacked his business cards back in the corner. He watched as I did this and then just walked away as if nothing happened. My mind still racing from what had just happened and I questioned myself. "Was it as bad as I thought or maybe it wasn't? Maybe it was just a misunderstanding." I walked down the hall to my son's room and opened the door. He looked at me with anger, fear, and disappointment and then shouted, "Where were you? I was scared!" Crying I said, "I'm sorry. I didn't realize or maybe was not processing what or why he was saying those things to you." For my own validation I asked him, "Did you seriously think your father was going to hit you?" He responded with tears, "Yes." I hugged him and said, "I'm going to fix this." At that moment I realized I was done trying.

The next morning he was lingering around the house. He was supposed to fly that evening so he did not go into work until late afternoon. I was quiet and short with my answers and responses to him. He knew something was wrong; he was clueless though. He had no idea why I was upset and quiet. He finally asked the question I had prepared myself for all night long. "What's wrong?" I responded by telling him I would tell him exactly what was wrong but that he was going to listen and this was not turning into a "poor him" session. He was not turning this around to be about him. I was not going to allow that this time. I felt scared but maternally defensive and ready to battle him for my children's sake. He agreed that he would listen. I told him that I was so tired. I told him that all I did was try to make life better for him and it was still not working. I said that I had no one to turn to and that I could not tell anyone that he was suffering inside in fear of damaging him publicly. I stated that the kids and I felt as though we walked around on eggshells, and we could not wait for the next work trip so that he would go away. I told him I was exhausted from the anger issues he had and I was trying constantly to smooth it out for him. I told him it was not normal to get angry about stuff that happens daily. It was life. I told him he no longer knew how to have fun and that he did not smile anymore. I had spent the last six years praying him better and trying to put the smile back on his face. All this by doing nothing but what he wanted and excluding myself, and the kids at times, in the process. I told him he ignored my cries for him to get help and how he would look at me as though I meant nothing to him. I told him that I was no longer in love with him and that I just felt obligated to him. I said, "If you do not get help soon, your children will feel the same way about you." He said nothing . . . he walked over to the phone, called, and was assigned a therapist that day.

 A night or two later, my daughter and I were asleep in my bed. My husband had forcefully opened our bedroom door and approached our closet. Having been asleep, his entrance awakened me and the light coming from the closet highlighted his actions. I witnessed him taking our handgun from its case and he had begun to load it. When I asked him what he was doing, he was delayed in his response. With no eye contact he said to me "Stay here." I dismissed his order and followed him down the hall. I asked him for a second time, "What are you doing?" I received no response from him. With his back to me he stopped at my son's bedroom and reached for the handle. I felt instant panic and I started to shake as my mind flashed to the whole drawer incident with my son just days before. I did not know if he was sleepwalking, dreaming, or just had lost all mental capabilities of thinking correctly. I shouted this time. "What are you doing?" He spoke only to my sleeping son. His words were "get into your mother's room." My heart sank as I walked back to my room with my son and closed the door. I did not know what he was doing or where he had gone, I just knew I had both my children with me and at that point it was all I cared about. A few minutes passed and he appeared at the bedroom door. I asked him to tell me what had just happened. He stated that he, while sleeping on the couch, heard a noise coming from our garage. All had checked out well and he returned the gun to its case. I could not sleep after that and for good reason. I was ashamed and frightened by my first thoughts when I had seen my husband reach for my son's door. Never should a mother think that the father of her children would ever do harm to them. I did. I did not know his state of mind and I had jumped to the worst conclusion ever. Besides the unwillingness to explain why he had the gun, he in all was just protecting his family. I do feel paranoia played a role in this. We lived in a safe neighborhood and our home was fully armed. No alarms had been tripped. I never shared my extreme thoughts about that night with him. After that though, I knew we were in trouble as a family and not only did he need help, but we all did.

 He started seeing a therapist weekly and at the beginning it was going well. I could see him trying hard with the kids. He tried to stay in the same room with them, controlling his responses to them and looking at me for affirmation and praise when he knew he had done well. I told him he was doing well and gave him the praise he seemed to have needed. With me, he jumped all in. He told me he loved me and that he was going to fix this. He said he was sorry and that all this was his fault. He stated that he mistreated me and neglected our family and that he was going to fight to get it all back. Did I fall into his arms and proclaim my love for him? Nope. I was pretty sure that is what he expected though. This way he could move on. He was retiring and he had things to do. He was in the process of applying for jobs and transitioning out of the army. Therapy and family issues would be in the way. If you knew him the way I knew him, yes this needed to be taken care of quickly.

He was attending his sessions weekly and working on his relationship with the kids and would often come home from session and tell me some of what his therapist would say. He seemed to be on spot and I liked the approach he was taking with my husband. I did ask often if they had started talking about Iraq. His response was always "No." I had wondered why that was and when he was going to start talking about the deployments. Very curious to find out what approach the therapist was taking with my husband, I accepted an invitation to participate in a three-way phone call. I was asked to tell of events that I felt detrimental to our marriage and family. I spoke of all major events leading up to his phone call for help. The one thing I did not share with the therapist was his Korea tour and his hurtful words to me during a painful time in my life. I held back. I did not know if I held back because it was embarrassing, or that I was still protecting him.

A few months into therapy and there had still been no talk of Iraq. They just spoke of his childhood and family history. I did ask him again why he was not talking about Iraq. He responded, "He doesn't think my issues stem from deployment." He would return home, at times, and share with me what had happened in his session. He said to me once that his therapist said there was nothing wrong with him and that there were plenty of women out there that would take him just as he is. He also repeated legal advice that his therapist supposedly shared with him about what a wife was actually entitled to if he were to divorce me. All of this he said was advised from his therapist and that it was what they talked about in session. He stated that the therapist knows this, because he himself was separated from his wife due to deployments. I knew listening to him speak these words to me that all that supposed therapy was for nothing. His financial worries, about to retire, looking for a job: all this was never talked about. I asked him why he was not sharing with him what he had shared with me. Why was he not telling him what he was worried about and above all what he had went through emotionally in Iraq. He said to me "I don't want to be lectured by him." I knew that! He now had the therapist thinking he was amazing and wonderful with just a few normal family issues. This therapist patted him on the back with each session and told him how great he was and how well he was doing and even went as far as to say that his marital issues were probably his wife's issues . . . perhaps how she was raised. All this he was more than happy to share with me. I do not know if his therapist actually said all of that, but I was not about to sit back and take it. I accepted yet another invitation that was extended to me, a few weeks prior, to sit in session with my husband. During this time I told everything and held nothing back. I told him how political my husband could be. He shook hands, gave his time and huge smiles to everyone in public, but behind closed doors he was a deeply depressed and unhappy individual. Neither the children nor I made him happy anymore. I told him of the years of covering for him lying to everyone and how lonely my life had become because of it. It took all my being to then tell him of the time I was told I possibly could have been dying. I then spoke of my husband and very best friend's refusal to give me a phone number to his room. When I needed him the most, he did not want me to bother him. The therapist was silent for a second then turned to him and said, "What I am about to say is going to be rough. You need to take time to process this. You have put your family in a jar. When you need them you take them out. When you don't, you put them back in." He in that moment put into words what my feelings had been for the past six years. My husband began to tear up and get emotional. The therapist asked him if he loved me and he responded, "Yes. I would not be here if I didn't love her." He asked him as a wife where did she fail. He responded, "She didn't. She has been the perfect wife she has done nothing wrong." Through it all though the whole session never once did I hear how great he was or that our issues stemmed from me or the way I had been raised. It was odd. I was expecting a battle and it was anything but. In fact his therapist put to words what emotionally I had been feeling for so long. Could it be possible that my husband was lying to me after his sessions? Could he have told me highlights of therapy and only what he wanted me to know? Yes, he could have, but there was nothing I could do about that.

A few days later I received a handwritten letter from my husband.

> To: My wife
>
> I know that I have not made your life easy in the last few years. You were absolutely correct when you said that you deserve better. I will do better and win your heart back! I realize that I have a lot to overcome from past woes, but you are worth it. You are asking why this now? Why didn't you do this five or six years ago? The old adage

of you don't realize what you have until it's gone, applies. The last few weeks I have tried to imagine all my future plans without you and I cannot. You are so entwined in my thoughts and plans for the future it hurts beyond belief to imagine that I screwed up so badly that you may never return to my side. What I am saying with this letter is, I will listen more than I speak. Not just listen but hear you. Compliment you not because it is what a book said but because I feel it in my heart. Realize that I am not just doing chores of work but I am doing things that you need done and trust me to do. Finally let me say this, I know you are not going to come running back into my arms with a piece of paper and some ink on it. Let this be a step back to winning your heart. I have never stopped loving you! You are my one and only. If I have to spend the rest of my life keeping you happy, it will be with love not a chore in my heart.

       Love . . . and then signed his name

Writing was never his high point. Pulling reference from a marital book his therapist recommended at the beginning of his therapy and the letter itself being slightly self-centered, he made the effort. "*My* future plans," not ours but his. Again omitted me. Also the end where he states "*if I have to*," this really got to me. I would have loved "if you'll let me" or a simple "I want to." I did not know what to think. Having told me, after each session, of legal advice, pats on the back and even blame laid on me by his therapist, I now had a letter telling me he could not imagine life without me. I was so confused.

Following his next session, he returned home and told me that his therapist wanted to try REM therapy. It was a therapy used to help soldiers coming back pinpoint their anxiety and where it was coming from. He was excited about this. He said, "I hope this works and they can fix me." Not knowing what was going on, in his session, I could only assume we were back to something was wrong with him and hope for the best from this treatment he was about to start. I had questions I did not ask. Were they now talking about Iraq, deployment, and what emotions he dealt with because of it? I had no clue.

The day arrived where he was to try the REM therapy. He was nervous but eager. He returned home and I asked him how it went. He looked at me as though he had no clue what I was asking him about. I said, "The REM therapy how did it go?" He said, "Oh, I didn't do that." I asked him why. He responded, "Because there is nothing wrong with me; I'm not doing that." And then he walked away. My mind was spinning and I had no clue what was going on. I could only watch, listen, and accept what he told me. I made the decision that I would start marriage counseling with him. I felt I needed to so that I could figure out what was happening.

I had approached my husband the next day and told him I wanted to start marriage counseling. Thinking he would say, "This is great. Let's do this." However, I heard the opposite. He said blankly, "No, I'm not doing that. I'm tired of being told what I did wrong. I just want to go away." He told me he was offered a job overseas and had accepted it. He was done and no longer had to try.

After accepting the job overseas, he went from locking me out of our joint checking account to letting me back in and taking nothing. He just left us. I believe he walked away with twenty dollars in his pocket. That was all he took with him. He promised to be there financially for us and to this day has never faulted on that. He filed for divorce and seven months after leaving, we were final.

I blamed myself, somewhat, for the destruction of my family. I felt I should have been stronger and spoken up about his emotional deterioration and physical separation from us. I did what I was told to do in an obedient manner. I felt double slammed though. As a Baptist-raised evangelical woman, I was brought up that you were to support and stand behind your husband at all cost. You were to support him through everything. Never were you to speak ill of him to others or demean him in any way . . . I didn't. As a military wife, you were encouraged to do the same. Stand by your soldier, support him, never stand in the way, and do not say anything or do anything that may reflect badly on him . . . I did just that.

I have a lot of questions and still no answers. How can four overseas tours (two of them being combative) take a person and change them so much that a twenty-three-year marriage and two beautiful kids were no longer anything to fight for. His country, the army . . . those he fought for. He poured his mind body and soul into fighting that war, but when it came to us, his family, we were not worth the fight. I felt as though we were disposable and thrown away. We were cast aside and he went off to start a new life on his own.

He now has a text and phone relationship with his children. My son, a very forgiving adult, speaks to him often. My daughter is still working through the anger she has from his effortless departure and inconsistent answers as to why he left. He told my son that he messed up but he just could not fix it and that he left his mom to make her happy. He later told my daughter that him leaving had nothing to do with them (meaning the kids), that he just did not love their mom anymore. It was all still very inconsistent. He told others we divorced because we grew apart. He grew apart, I held on for six years. He never speaks about the night he went after our son and how terrifying it was. In reality, that night set in motion the ending of our family.

I am torn because I know we need good soldiers and my ex-husband was one of the very best. Building that soldier, that super being, was at the cost of our family. I find it hard to stand or sit through a public solute to our soldiers or a public welcome home . . . its gut wrenching to think what might be happening after that welcome home.

In an Instant . . . He Was Gone

There are those who serve in the military and there are those who serve for the military. Both types of service being honorable but personally viewed differently. Serving in the military, you are assigned a job; you do this job and collect your paycheck. It is a job you have while searching for other opportunities and counting down to the day you are released back into the civilian world. When you serve for the military, it is a passion, belief, and a way of life. It is your career and you consider nothing less than your twenty years of service.

My husband definitely served for the military. It was never a question as to whether or not he would serve his full twenty years of service. I knew he was a career military man and I was right there, by his side, and with him every step of the way.

Throughout his twenty years in service, I had devoted myself to supporting him. I did not just support him but I devoted time and effort to the military also. I was extremely proud to call myself an "army wife" and to wear the stigma that came along with that title. I had involved myself in the FRG (Family Readiness Group), bonded and connected with other spouses, and kept actively involved during "our" twenty years of service.

As the military became more and more a part of our lives, pieces of my husband went away and the man I knew prior to the military faded. Our lives changed with his service in Kuwait (Dessert Storm) and his career came to an end with a deployment to Iraq. Never did I realize that training, deployments, and war itself had the capability to change a loving husband and father so much that he would no longer be recognizable.

Early in my husband's career, he had routinely attended military courses and training. The saying "here today, gone tomorrow" was not just a saying; we lived it every day. It was what I had grown to expect from his job and what I knew as normal for a soldier in the army. We became accustomed to it and time apart was short lived and tolerable. Every return home was a welcome event, and life from duty station to duty station was routinely the same.

His first deployment in a combat zone was to Kuwait (Dessert Storm). Communication was scarce and phone calls were few and far between. Waiting was hard but I considered myself lucky. I could not imagine what the wives of our past wars went through when letter writing was the only form of communication. So I waited and presented myself as patient. Knowing he was in a war zone made being patient that much harder. I did exactly what was expected of me as a military wife. I took care of our home, our child, and waited to hear from him.

His deployment to Kuwait was not very eventful. If it was, I was told nothing about it. He returned from Kuwait and we had orders immediately to Hawaii. It is quite rare that we had gotten such a highly requested duty station. For him to have received orders to Hawaii, right after serving in a war zone, seemed to be such a healing and kind life change. It was exactly that . . . so I thought. Now I look back and think it was more of a suppression of what would later rear its ugly head.

While in Hawaii, family time, our marriage, and life together was just as anticipated. It was fun, enjoyable, and having obtained orders to Hawaii could not have worked out better for us. After serving in a warzone, he was living on an island with his wife and child. He seemed happy, content, and as a family, "grateful" would have described us.

Upon completion of our tour in Hawaii, we were sent stateside again. That is when life with my husband immediately changed. It changed quickly and he was, without a doubt, different. What I could not quite put into words before, I can now say it was like flipping a light switch.

We had our second child and he had made rank (E-7) shortly after. When a soldier makes "rank," completion of an extensive amount of training and courses go along with that promotion. Training that lasted months and large spans of time away from the family were expected. Prior to E-7, he had been airborne and separation from us was frequent. Arriving home at 3:00 a.m. or being called in at 2:00 a.m. was quite normal. He would, at times, be gone all night and I never questioned it. That was his job and I accepted that. With the promotion came more intense training. Having had two children at that point, things at home started to decline.

There were noticeable changes in my husband's behavior. He had distanced himself from me and anger had taken over his passive demeanor. I once stood in our hall, peering into the living room, just watching him. He had returned from a training mission and was sitting on our couch messing with his military equipment. He was trying to fix his helmet (Kevlar) but like "flipping a switch" frustration came over him and anger soon overwhelmed him. He stood up, took his helmet, and hurled it across the room. It impacted the wall and fell to the floor. He stood there, alone in the room. His breathing was heavy and his body tense. I continued to watch as he just stood there staring at his helmet on the floor. He did not know I had witnessed his outburst or that I was even there. I focused on him, keeping my eyes on him and trying to reason in my own mind why he would do such a thing. It was one of the first demonstrated bouts of anger from him that frightened me. I knew that he was mentally dealing with something that day, an inner struggle of some sort. I could see it in his face, his actions, and reactions. Sometime after, he approached me and said he did not think he wanted to be married anymore. He stated that I no longer knew who he was. I said nothing to him and responded with silence. I stood there listening as though this were someone other than my husband speaking to me. This was not the man I had known and loved. He never approached the subject with me again after that. I realized my husband was struggling with something and he had no control over it. I had no clue what it was but it was just the beginning and our life, as we knew it, would become a distant memory.

There were days that passed and I wondered who he was and then there were days he seemed perfectly normal. I found myself missing the strong family man sitting in church on Sundays with his arms stretched out, lying across the top of pews and hands around our shoulders. He was proud of us and happy to be with us. I missed the man that enjoyed others and his family. His own mother witnessed a few of his outburst and commented on his actions. She stated to me that she often wondered why he was acting like that. We all could see he was changing but we were incapable of stopping it. My prayer was that it would just subside.

Years past and he had pulled it together mostly. He functioned well in his routine and I believed structure for him helped. As any great soldier would, he devoted most of his time and all of his efforts to the job he had. He was in his element while at work and completed his daily missions. The army should have been thrilled to have a soldier serve for them the way he did. My husband knew no other way than to give 100 percent to them.

Life for us became nonstop training with his deployment orders to Iraq. We never really saw him but in passing so, communication was little if at all between us. Nothing changed; his focus was and always had been on the mission. He was continuously gone training for that deployment and then ultimately off to Iraq.

The relationship, while he was deployed, was a distant one. I did not get to speak to him but once a month, at the most. The kids never spoke with him. When he did call, he always asked to speak to me. He no longer cared to talk to them. It was hurtful to them, but I continuously spoke kindly and stated to them that their dad was extremely busy and had very few free moments. It was a lonely year and we were struggling as a couple. I still kept trying to be his good wife and sole supporter back home. There was only so much he would accept from me though.

His return home was not a joyful event and was filled with turmoil and uncertainty. Upon his return from Iraq he was forced into retirement, by the army, due to an affair with a female soldier in a combat zone. He did not care what he had done or that I even knew about it. He continued his destructive actions and behavior right in front of the children and me. He would e-mail her and the words "I love you" were all throughout the e-mails. All of this was done in front of my third grader who was fully capable of reading. He did not care. He did not even try to hide it. It was not just the female he met during deployment, but he was doing that with whomever he could find in town. He could not stop. He would pursue them on the phone, in my presence, knowing that I was aware of what he was doing. He would speak to these women in front of me; at times, in front of my children, while I was gone. When I would confront him about it, he would say that he was not stopping, that he could not stop. He refused, as though it were some sort of illness. He was going to do what he wanted to do, and I was just going to have to put up with it. That was his attitude and his demeanor. It was a type of arrogance and defiance, and I was the one dealing with it.

I made the decision to try my best to hold onto my marriage and bring my husband back to us. I assume others would have given up and walked away; I still remembered the loving husband, father, and son he used to be. I wanted him back. Not knowing what approach I should take to bring him back to us, I did what I thought made sense. I would randomly walk up behind him and wrap my arms around him. I would hold on so tight in hopes of loving him enough to bring him back. He would, without expression or words, unclutch my arms and shove me away. He was a wall. There was no breaking through that barrier he had put up around himself. I did not stop though. I continued at times to walk up to him and hold on. Sometimes, he would respond with a slight smile or hug. Those were the times I saw the man he used to be. He quickly retreated though, and those moments were suffocated by whatever he was battling mentally.

Socially, we retreated and as a family we did not participate in much of anything. Activities outside the home were few and far between. He was socially awkward and unexpressive. There were days when he would open up and speak to me like he used to . . . then he would mentally retreat. He would, sadly, sink back into that place in his head; a place that I often wondered about. I knew by his expressionless appearance, he stayed there most of the time.

In a "normal" state, he would share with me that he had moments where he would "black out" and that he could not remember. I would remind him of conversations we had and he would tell me he did not remember having them or what he said during them. He said he felt like he had blank spaces in his head and did not know what was supposed to be there. He also stated to me that he thought he might be suicidal. He said that while hunting, sitting there alone in the deer stand, he had often thought about turning the gun around. He said there were times when he did look down the barrel. He said that thought entered his head a lot.

He was no longer sleeping at night and would hear voices in his head that would keep him awake. Often he would be up all night sick in the bathroom but never enough that he wanted or was willing to seek help. I begged him but he was not getting help no matter what. I assumed that was a military thing. They know there is something wrong with them but refused to seek help. In his eyes, that would have been a sign of weakness. He never showed weakness. He was a true soldier when he served and strength was part of his mental and physical make up. Sadly, I could see his "strength" was destroying him.

His anger became violent and his illness was apparent. The children and I lived in fear and we were afraid of him most days. Love or the ability to even care, no longer existed in this man. He had turned into a man unable to give or receive any affection. I tried hard to push him into caring but my efforts were suspended with his words . . . "I don't love you. I don't love the kids. I don't love anybody. I don't know why you love me. I don't know why the kids love me." He saw no reason to exist.

He became very aggressive verbally and physically. One evening, that I will remember always, I came to the realization that he had no regard for me or any other human. I had returned home from work, walked in the door, and asked how things were going. Looking at me, he stood straight up, forcefully picked up his cell phone and went to throw it at me. When he reared back, he slung it and it flew in the opposite direction. The force of his throw was so strong that the phone actually penetrated the wall. My daughter was shaking and screaming at the sight of phone protruding out of the wall and the thought that he had originally intended for it to hit me. He had no reaction or remorse for what he had done. Shortly after, his family came to the house and asked what had happened to the wall. He was still expressionless and had no remorse about the incident. In recalling it, he blamed me for provoking him. I assumed because I came home, walked through the house, and asked how things were going. It made no sense to me or to them.

His anger and aggression was affecting our children. These children tried so hard to love him and be loved by him. He was the first one they wanted to include in their lives and in return, wanted to be included by him. An assignment, assigned to my son, was to interview a veteran. I myself never understood this type of assignment. Most veterans do not like to speak about their war experiences and he was not about to either. There was no way he would ever open up like that. The first person my son wanted to interview was his dad. He was proud of his father's service as he was told he should be. At my son's request for an interview, my husband refused. It became a huge ordeal that left my son crying and I ended up doing the interview myself. He wanted nothing to do with that and refused to even speak of it. Prior to asking him, I already knew he would refuse. He never spoke of his time deployed or answered questions about what he experienced over there. There was only one time that I could recall that he shared with me an incident that happened while deployed. He was "cleanup" after a group of enemy had been destroyed. He had called in their position, they were destroyed and he was part of the team that had to clean up their bodies. Upon recalling this, he was emotional and very shaken physically. He never spoke of it again. That was the only time he had ever shared any part of his deployments with me. He spoke of nothing else pertaining to his wartime or what took place during it.

He was so violent that hiding his anger and actions became impossible; my family witnessed this first hand. My sister and her family came for a visit and were staying with us. One morning, my son was sitting in the kitchen, eating. My husband, in another room, was watching TV. In a random moment of anger and rage-filled voice, he stated that my son was making too much noise. He proceeded to the kitchen, picked my son up by his hair, dragged him through the house and down the hall. The only sound was my son screaming as he held onto him by nothing but his hair. My family was paralyzed by fear, as was I. I composed myself quickly and thought fast in order to save my son. I walked down the hall, opened the door, and looked him straight in the eye. I then played a dangerous game. His intent was to beat him, but with determination and a solid voice I spoke the words "I'll take care of him . . . let me take care of him," as though I was going to administer the beating myself. Slowly and determined, I repeated, "I'll do it . . . you just go and let me do it." As he let go of him, my son dropped to the floor and husband walked out of the room. Somehow I had convinced him that I was going to continue what he had started. Normally, I would have been a spitfire and said, "Don't touch him." He was not "normal" though and I had to approach the situation in a totally different manner. I swallowed hard and held my son as my husband retreated to another room. He stayed there, away from all of us, for the rest of the night. My son was in the fifth grade at that time. It still frightens me to think about what might have happened that morning. I feel very blessed to have saved my child from a horror that only my mind could imagine.

It had been a year after his deployment to Iraq, and I was still trying to bring him back to "normal" on my own. I sat with my pastor and he said to me that he had never seen someone so empty and blank, referring to my husband. He, at one point, tried counseling with my pastor and had no success. The children were now all seeing a therapist and we, as a couple, were seeking therapy. I do not know why he agreed to see a therapist. Our therapist said at the beginning if he did not see any improvement or progress that he would dismiss us. He did not want to waste his time, our time, and our money. After six weeks of seeing our therapist, my husband was still doing as he pleased. The therapist told him he felt sorry for him and that he was dismissing us. He told him he had no interest in being there or doing the work to improve our situation. He offered to individually see us, but as a couple he would not. My husband was furious about being dismissed. I can only assume he wanted therapy so I would continue to let him live with us. As long as I saw him continuing to see the therapist, I would see that he was trying. He felt that he could do as he pleased and say he was trying. I could no longer continue life that way and I let him go.

I started the process of doing what I needed to do to keep my family safe. He was distant, secretive, and vile. He would often come home in the middle of the night. I always had the children in bed with me, in my room and behind a locked door. We were afraid of him and what he may do next. We would see him in passing, and most nights he slept in another room. I was done trying to fix him and concluded that I could not fix him on my own.

I made the decision to divorce my husband. I had known him since we were teenagers and loved him for a greater part of our lives. The decision to divorce did not come easy but was justified. My husband no longer existed and this man we feared. When I filed for divorce, he was livid. The person that served him his divorce papers stated that he frightened them while in the process of being served. I feel he was upset at the loss of his "cover." With us he could convince himself that everything was normal and that he was OK. He looked good on the outside and that was important. He was making his life look perfect to everyone else while suffering silently.

He left our home and moved in with a friend and his wife for a while. He had become so violent that he was ordered to see a therapist in order to get a clean bill of mental health. He was forced to do this so that he would be permitted to see the children. He had lost control and everyone saw it.

Two weeks before our divorce, he called me and told me that I had to let him come home. He said that the police were chasing him and that they were going to put him in jail. I responded, "Where is home? This hasn't been your home in a long time and I'm not letting you come back, especially in the state that you are in." We divorced two weeks later, and roughly two weeks after that, he was arrested for beating up his girlfriend. He was released from jail and was arrested again for kidnapping a twenty-three-year-old girl and brought up on assault and battery charges. He lost all control of himself and was a danger to others.

He no longer has contact with our children. After his first arrest, I had filed a restraining order. However, the judge refused to sign it. The judge stated to my lawyer that he just did this divorce two weeks prior and he was not signing it. Shortly after, my ex-husband was brought into the courtroom. His demeanor was agitated and violent. After a few questions and short conversation with our judge, the judge then reversed his decision and signed the restraining order.

Jailed over a year for continued beatings of the same girl, I felt like the kids and I merely escaped that horror. I felt like the kids and I were his sanity . . . that as long as he was in this home and had his family, he was OK in his head. After the divorce, after he lost us, nothing else mattered to him. He no longer cared. He did not have to. To this day, he continues to exhibit destructive behavior. I still have the authorities contact me trying to find out where he is and hoping I can help them locate him. With every request, my response to them is the same, "I have no clue." I have had strange men walk up to me in parking lots and in front of my home to ask me where he is. I always respond with "I don't know." I have gotten in my car and strangers watch me from across the street or parking lot. It is frightening and unsettling. I do not know what he has been up to or what he deals with. I did everything I could to try to save our marriage and our family. I was willing to accept him in anyway, forgiving anything he had done as long as he was willing to come back to us as a father and a husband. He refused and always reinforced that he did not love the children or me.

Training, pressures of the job, and deployment changed the man I married. I think with constant rotation of commanders, it would have been impossible for them to recognize he was suffering. There was not enough time from one commander to the next to get to know him and to determine that he needed help. I was angry with the army for failing one of their best soldiers. He served them for twenty years and did exactly what he was trained to do. He lost his family, friends, and mental stability.

My feelings toward veterans have changed. I have a hard time going to a Veteran's Day parade without getting upset. My children, sadly, feel the same way. My son's refusal to write a paper on veterans and all the great things about them spoke volumes as to how he felt about his father and the label "veteran." He said he was not writing it, that he could not stand veterans and that he wanted nothing to do with them. His feelings all stemmed from his father, his friend's fathers, and my friend's husbands. They did not just see it in their own father but they watched others self-destruct too. My children felt like the army took their dad from them . . . I do not blame them.

In one of my last conversations with him, I told him he never came back from over there. I think he already knew that.

Entitled

Some say that love at first sight is perhaps a mistaken emotion for infatuation and that it could not possibly be "love." Others say it is an emotional visual experience that grabs hold of you and will not let go. Whether you believe in the possibility or not, there are those that say that is exactly how it happened for them.

Walking across a crowded parking lot one day, a soldier glanced at female soldier and in an instant he knew he would one day marry her. I happened to have been that female soldier. We were both enlisted, serving our country, and happened to be stationed in Germany at the same time. He said he knew he was going to marry me from the moment he laid eyes on me. It was a very dramatic and exaggerated statement, but after meeting and dating him, I believed his "love at first sight" story to be truthful.

At the time of his "first sighting," I was involved with another soldier who was stationed stateside. We were dating long distance and trying our best to hold up a relationship. We talked about getting married and had thrown the idea around a few times. I being a young and immature nineteen-year-old decided to do just that. I flew back to the States and I married him. This turned out to be a huge mistake, and the marriage was very short-lived.

When I returned to Germany, I found it difficult to get in contact with him. He was rarely available. When I would call back to the states, I was told he was at the beach celebrating or my phone calls were completely ignored. I found myself married to a man who had limited my communication with him and when I did have the opportunity to speak with him, the conversations were short ended. I, still nineteen and very young, made another decision. I decided that if he was not into this marriage, I was not going to be either. Still legally married to this man, we ended up just going our separate ways. I dated, he dated, and we really no longer had contact with each other.

After a very romantic pursuit of me, I started dating the man that fell for me at first sight. I knew instantly he wanted to be with me. It was like nothing I had ever felt before, not even with my estranged husband. It was unbelievable to me, the difference from one man to another. He was attentive, loving, caring, and when I was with him, I felt like I was on top of a pedestal and he was the one that placed me there. The time I spent with him was not wasted. We fell in love and knew we would be together for life.

After a year of dating, I became pregnant with our son. I knew I needed to finally dissolve my marriage and so, I did just that. With the help of a family attorney, my marriage was annulled and I was no longer tied to that man and mistake I had made early on.

I, a soldier, was PCS-ing (being reassigned) stateside and father of my baby was still assigned to a base in Germany. We corresponded via phone and letters and again, I found myself in a long-distance relationship. It was different though. He loved me, wanted to talk to me and hear about our pregnancy; this made a world of difference. I knew he loved me and I was in love him.

He soon PCS-ed stateside and we were able to continue our relationship. With a baby on the way and finally back together, marriage was our next step. We married just before making the move to our next duty station. We were truly happy and very excited to start our life together. Upon arriving to our new duty station and with the arrival of our son, I started the process of separating from the army. This would enable me to stay home with and care for our baby. My husband had joined a new unit and was gone one to two weeks out of the month. This was very hard. With his absence, it was just my son and I. Looking back; this is how it had been our whole marriage . . . just my son and I.

The first ten years of our marriage were rough, financially. We struggled and had very little money. I remember at one point wrapping up nickels to buy baby formula. I have to say during that long rough patch, he never failed me. He treated me awesome. I was still everything he ever wanted. Life's struggles never affected his love for me, and we remained strong in our marriage. We had mutual respect for each other, and the love he had for me was returned ten times over. We truly had a working marriage, and we loved our little family.

With the exception of his monthly training, he had not been away from us for very long periods of time. His first deployment to Korea would take him away for a year. I know it is not considered a deployment but unless you are able to go with them, they go by themselves and it feels like a deployment. If the family goes with them, it is twenty-four months, but in some cases this is not even an option for the family. So most choose not to go and just do the year apart with a thirty day visit home sometime during that year. We chose the year apart.

He was only in Korea for four months when he was sent to the Philippines. During this time they had an aircraft go down and six men died in that crash. It was his job to help recover their bodies. After that incident, he was not provided or offered the assistance of a chaplain, counselor, or anyone else that could of helped him mentally deal. What he and his fellow soldiers had experienced, losing these men and having to recover their bodies, had to be mind tolling. These were the bodies of his coworkers, brothers, and friends. This is what they had become to each other while serving together. Normal everyday people do not experience this sort of situation, and he himself had not until that point. Adding to that permanent mental visual, the incident took place on our son's birthday. A day that he should always rejoice in had become the day he will forever remember recovering the bodies of his military brothers.

He finished out his time in Korea and then returned home to us. He was his loving kind self and very happy to be back with us. Upon his return, the unit he was assigned to happened to be in route to Iraq and he was on the list to go with them. Six months after his return from Korea, he was on his way to Iraq. It was the scariest time ever for both of us. We could not speak to each other for two weeks. I did not know what was going on and he could not tell me anything. He had finally arrived at their assigned destination and the war was in full swing. Everything broke bad and it did very quickly. Communication was extremely limited. It was not until after six months into his rotation over there that they finally got viable communication going. This made life miserable on both of us and taxed us mentally almost daily.

He was moving up in the ranks fairly quickly over there. He was an E-6 when they deployed and got picked up for E-7 when they arrived in Iraq. We were doing better financially and to add to that, he was on his way home to us. I was excited and extremely relieved upon his return. Welcoming him and the rest of his unit home was a fulfilled moment in a long anticipation. I felt like our life could now resume and the terrifying wait had ended.

My husband arrived home and things were great. We were excited about being together as a family, again. We did stuff together daily. Cooking, cleaning, playing, these are things that nonmilitary families did every day and take for granted. We looked at these task and moments as special, and the time spent together was appreciated. We took a trip to the islands and spent quality time together. We were overwhelmed mentally at the fact that we were together and that he had made it back to us safely. What seemed to be such a short time after the welcome home, the training started again . . . then came Iraq deployment number two. The second deployment to Iraq was the beginning of our lives being turned upside down.

When my husband deployed yet a second time to Iraq, I took a job on base just to help pass time and keep my mind off what may be going on over there. It is hard for us as wives to deal with life back here. When you have a free moment, your mind tends to go there, there with them: wondering, worrying, and guessing what may or may not be happening. So, I wanted to fill in as much free time as I could to keep from thinking about it. My husband never understood why I took the job. Maybe he could not relate to what I was going through over here because he was too busy trying to relate to what he was going through over there. All I knew was it was a very long year, and I needed to keep busy.

My husband completed yet another year in Iraq and was on his way home. I had anticipated the same reunion as the last and my excitement was topped out. He returned home and it was just as I had hoped for. We could not get enough of each other and being together was an absolute "honeymoon." I know why so many military wives refer to it as the "honeymoon phase." A phase was exactly what it turned out to be.

He quickly turned from a man grateful to be home and with his family to an angry and often hateful, agitated person. We battled for time, attention, and his love. He was separating mentally and physically from us, and our presence in his life became daily obstacles. Arguments came often and blame was always laid upon me. Never would he accept blame or fault. It was always me. Even if I were not involved in a problem he was having, he would find a way to make that problem my fault. He was combative and not loving at all. This man that was returned home to us was not my husband. I was struggling daily and hoping for some kind of relief from his mental state. I was coping to the best of my ability and wondering what happened. I was in shock at the life I was leading with him at this point and to top it all off, a deployment to Afghanistan was upon us.

He was a first sergeant and in charge of roughly 120 soldiers. He took his job very seriously. He knew these guys would leave together, and he wanted to ensure that they came home together. Because of this, I witnessed a lot of pressure on him prior to deployment. I knew he felt the pressure here stateside, so I could not imagine how he would feel once he had arrived in theater (assignment in Afghanistan). The training and the pressures behind it, I felt aided in impairing the decisions he made and his view of what were priorities. All this I dealt with first hand and hoped it would not affect his ability to lead over there.

My son was a teenager and struggling with normal teenage stuff, if you add the fact that his dad was in a war zone repeatedly while growing up, you could conclude that he was not a stress-free child. It took its toll on him just as it did myself. During a routine visit to the doctor, for a routine sports physical, the doctor pulled me aside and told me she felt my son might need to talk to someone and suggested a therapist that could help him. After waiting for communication from my husband, he called and I told him of the doctor's suggestion for our son. He firmly said no to me. He stated that if our son were to see a therapist, it would ruin his career. His career, not my son's future, but his. He somehow thought this could have been perceived as a weakness in his family and would reflect badly upon him. My son struggling with personal issues that no teenage boy should have to, and his own father was denying him help. My husband was not concerned about our son but the way others may view him and his family. It was all about him. He had put his career above his son's well-being. I wondered, how much more were we to sacrifice, as a family for him?

He was in the middle of his deployment to Afghanistan and he had decided (to himself) that he was not going to stay married. He had planned that when he returned, he was making his way out and leaving us. I did not realize this until months after his return home. He kept up communication with me and continued to be my deployed husband, but all along he wanted out. He did not want to be married or be part of our family anymore. All of his feelings and self-made plans he kept to himself while deployed.

When he returned home from his deployment, he told me that he had dropped his retirement paperwork while overseas and that he was done doing this. During the process of retiring, I noticed more anger, bitterness, and hatefulness, all of it so purposeful. Nothing was ever right and I was to blame. Alcohol played a main roll in his life and signs of PTSD were made very apparent. He was unable to sleep and therefore took sleeping pills. He was verbally abusive to our son and me. This had become worse with each return from deployment. He was no longer content and his life was not good enough anymore. The job was not good enough, the family he had was not good enough, and he wanted out. I was living with a man that had emotionally shut down. He would answer no questions, had no comments or interaction, and he was quick to anger when pushed.

During his out-process part of retirement, he was given a physical and mental evaluation. During that evaluation, he was diagnosed with 50 percent PTSD. He was actually not offended by it and accepted the diagnosis. He informed me that he was not getting help for it and could collect more disability because of it. I did not think he would have ever sought help for it because he did not see it as a problem. He saw us as the problem and the life he was leading. I think he actually thought he deserved better than the wife he had and life with us.

Our relationship was suffering and his relationship with our teenage son was suffering. He decided that he wanted to take a job in another state. We discussed the pros and cons and decided that financially it would be a good move to leave my son and I here, and he take this job elsewhere. I had agreed to this only because we discussed it together and decided that it would be for the best. In a conversation soon after, he informed me he was only taking that job in order to get away from me. He stated that while in Afghanistan, he decided that he did not want to be married anymore, and that he wanted out. He looked at me with contempt and stated that this job was his way out. His statement of wanting out did not surprise me. After all he did a great job informing me through his actions and disconnect. I was not done yet though. I wanted him to remember loving me. I wanted him to remember the way he felt when he saw me for the first time. I was trying to hold on.

I was still struggling to hold onto him and our marriage. I was commuting to see him and he would often come home for long weekends. These weekends, that he would come home for, ended up being uncomfortable, stressful, and worthless. I would receive emotional shutdown and physical silence. The only thing he would speak to me about was his four deployments. He would often tell me how he was a rare soldier and that there are very few soldiers that had to do four deployments for their country. Bragging, he would state that he achieved what others had not. He felt entitled and he stated that he should reward himself and buy a brand new Corvette. I had to ask myself what kind of mental state was he functioning in to have had verbally expressed something like that. Telling me, not only his wife, but also a former soldier myself, that he should be rewarded with a brand new Corvette because he fought for our country and did it four times . . . unbelievable! I looked at him and stated firmly that he needed help. I told him that covering up was only destroying him and the little relationship he had left with his son.

His relationship with our son was so strained and had only gotten worse. Anger played a huge role in that. I remember driving down the road one time while he and my son argued. To this day, what happened next stills shocks me to think of it. The argument escalated and my husband let anger control him. While driving, he was able to reach over the front seats into the back and repeatedly beat my son who was sitting in the back seat. We were on the road, in a vehicle moving, and he was beating my son. All of this was done in uncontrollable anger. These are the moments, these are the incidents that destroy relationships, and he was mastering that.

He was starting to enjoy life at his new job living in a completely different state from his wife and son. He was meeting new people and now enjoying the company of younger women. One woman in particular he jokingly referred to as his work wife. When I became curious, I read the phone bill. There were two hundred and fifty texts in one month. These texts were between the two of them and at all hours of the night. Upon one of my visits there, I opened his phone and read some of them. It was all about me. He texted how much he wanted out and how I was to blame for every failure, and our failed marriage was my fault. I considered this an emotional affair with her and confronted him about it. He again blamed me and told me she listened to him. This woman told others she admired him and considered him a mentor. She was twenty-eight. He craved affirmation and ego strokes and she did that for him. It had not just been her though. He fed off praise from others too. His wife loving and respecting him was no longer enough . . . he needed something else and decided to go and get it.

 He stopped coming home on long weekends and participating in my son's sporting events. He requested that we split our finances and I refused. He then returned home and informed our teenage son that he would be divorcing me. He did this before he even spoke to me about it. He told me he was tired of arguing and wanted out. He stated that he was done being married and being here with us. Giving in and feeling I had lost him forever, I filed for legal separation. Separated from a man I knew at one time would protect, love, and care for me forever. Separated now from a man I no longer knew.

 The divorce process became a nightmare. I promised my son he would never hear me demean his father in front of him, yet my estranged husband accused me often of doing just that. I tried to communicate with him via text about problems our son was having and asked if he could come back to help. I asked if we could sit down and talk to our son as united parents. However, he never answered his phone or texts. He even went as far as to block my number. I in turn did the same. I realized that I was on my own with my son, just as I had always been. Weeks later, he tried to text me and realized I had blocked him. He then he accused me of keeping him from his son, a son he would not discuss or come back to help. I told him we did not need this anymore. I told him that my son and I did not want the drama and the inconsistency in our lives. He seemed very confused and self-centered. He refused spousal support, and anger was what fueled him.

He was totally different among others. He was the life of the party, joking, fun, and they could not get enough of him. Before deployments, he was home at night. He was a husband and father. We would entertain friends on weekends and he was good to them just as he was to us. Now my son and I were his worst enemies. We were his family, main support, and abundant amount of love. Now, he could not seem to get away fast enough. He traded us in for another life. This was life that consisted of drinking till memory loss, bragging about it, younger women, and nonstop partying. He felt he deserved more than us, and he left us to find what he felt he deserved.

I lost the man I married . . . the man I was in love with. I blamed the army for not giving him help he needed upon his return from deployments. I blamed him for not seeking the help he needed. All because he was afraid it would have shown weakness and he feared the backlash it may have had on his career. I lost deeply in this war and so did my son. My husband . . . he got a brand new life.

Closing

These soldiers came back missing and as their wives, we were left with unanswered questions. In a quest to understand what may have happened to these men, I found myself striking up conversation with random veterans at times. I did this often and wondered if I would ever key in on one thing that could have explained our loss. The opportunity presented itself to me a couple of times and I was able to speak to two different veterans who had returned from two different wars; two wars decades apart yet surprisingly, one main thing in common.

I was dining one evening, at a waterside tavern, when I encountered and was introduced to a Vietnam veteran. In a polite conversation I happened to share my personal story and he, in return, shared a little bit of his postwar life with me. With complete eye contact and a willingness to share he spoke of his return home and the changes in him that followed. His demeanor was calm but arrogantly confident while he told his story and what life was like for him after the war. He stated to me that upon his return, he was a very angry young man and that he was never able to pinpoint why. He said life was different when he came back and that anger controlled and dictated his actions. He spoke of a dissolved marriage and a distant relationship with his children. He said although he was now remarried, he was very aware of what drove him and how it was a battle daily. He, an older man in his sixties, said that he felt he still could have taken down, single handedly, anyone who decided to cross him. Thinking back on my own story, and the stories of others, I then posed a question to him. "Do you think that your anger, attitude, and demeanor played a key role in your survival and ability to carry out your mission while in a war zone?" He answered with a tilt to his head and with a seemingly recognizable realization in his expression . . . "Yes, yes it did."

In a visit to a historical town, I had been seated next to a man and a conversation evolved. He stated to me that he was a retired JAG (Judge Advocate General) officer and that his service was rendered in Iraq. He said although retired, he was now defending current soldiers and veterans accused of crimes due to PTSD. I again took the opportunity and shared my personal story with him. As he listened, it was as if he knew exactly what I was going to say next. With a constant nod of his head, he often finished some of my key sentences. When I concluded my story, he stated that the main issue he had been dealing with from the soldiers, he was defending, was anger. The word "anger" keyed me in, and I again posed a similar question to him that I had previously asked to the Vietnam veteran . . . "Do you think the anger, attitude, and demeanor of these returning soldiers is what helped them to survive war and carry out their mission?" He responded with a continuous head nod and with the word "absolutely."

These were two conversations from two different veterans from two different parts of the US. What struck me as unusual though; they were veterans from two different wars and yet agreed upon one main focus. One could only conclude that the same anger, narcissistic attitude, and invincible demeanor of these soldiers that kept them alive and helped them carry out their mission, is sadly the same thing that destroyed them and their families upon their return home.

Having worked for an institution that enforced security, structure, rule, and regulations were in deep play. This was rarely strayed from and reinforced daily to achieve and fulfill a mission. Upon their return home, life became demanding, nonstructured, and family life consisted of daily changes. Coping was difficult and was often confusing. We as wives witnessed this first hand.

The relationship between a soldier and his family was never consistent. The time they would spend with their family was limited from training to deployments. When some of these soldiers returned home, longer than normal, they could not seem to handle it. Some quit, some ran and others just lived in complete disarray. The question to ask is, "Why would they not have asked for help before turning their backs on the ones they loved so dearly?"

The families of these soldiers waited for, prayed for, and celebrated their return home. That return was the end to a daily ritual of fear and worry that had the ability to grab hold of you and not let go. It was not until they were able to lay eyes on their soldier and witness them safely on American soil that the fear would subside. Finally given the opportunity to physically wrap their arms around them gave way to a sea of emotions that they themselves were not prepared for. That reunion was long awaited, and for some it was the hopeful beginning of life again with the one loved and supported.

They deployed family men who were also soldiers prepared for a mission. They were returned to us angry, sad, and self-centered. Others returned with mental pain so deep that they themselves were unaware of its origin. These soldiers fought for their country, but upon their return refused to fight for their family. They sacrificed the ones they loved and the ones that loved them in order to carry out a mission . . . a mission that took them away and never returned them the same.

What happened that would make several people, in the same situation, participating in the same war, react so differently? Why did some come back and embrace their family and others retreated mentally. Were we missing something? What were they being told over there? Why was not more being done about the struggle of the returning soldier? Was our military doing enough for these soldiers? Did they help them to return home, to fit into their life again, to exist and function normally? Then again, maybe they did. Maybe it was the type of soldier they had bred. One that was strong physically and felt weak if mentally taxed. One that was afraid to ask for help from the same institution that stressed strength and readiness as a way of promoting a high-speed soldier in today's world.

As Americans, we needed great warriors to defend and fight for our country in a world where others were waiting to destroy us. These warriors stepped away from the security of their homes and families to fight and defend our nation. They were pushed to physical limits daily and mentally exhausted. They had given all they had to a war that did not seem to end . . . but were they dispensable?

I struggled personally with a question I posed to myself as an American and former military wife. As a commander running this war, would I have wanted to mentally remove them from the mission upon their return home? I would have to answer no. It would not have been productive. I would not have wanted to bring them back mentally when, in a year, I would have been sending them back to continue the mission. I would have actually wanted to keep them in that mindset for as long as possible so that their focus was on nothing else but the mission and its success. Now, as a former military wife, I wanted him back not only physically but also mentally. I wanted them to fix whatever was broken in him and return him to us the way he left us. One general auditorium lecture upon their return was not enough. I wanted a total individual evaluation upon each return and total top to bottom scan of what he had gone through over there. I wanted him back.

Through these stories, you have learned another side to the "Welcome Home." Sadly, it is a different version. For them, when the banners have been taken down, the balloons are gone, and life back home was to begin again . . . they were lost. Some took it in strides, others failed to fit in, and there were those that would not even try.

Those we stood behind, loved, respected, and cared for are also the ones we now feared, were hurt and betrayed by. It was not only us, but it was our children, our families, and our friends. A sad version of an American hero now exists.

Edwards Brothers Malloy
Thorofare, NJ USA
November 13, 2015